Just Get on the Pill

Reproductive Justice: A New Vision for the Twenty-First Century

EDITED BY RICKIE SOLINGER, KHIARA M. BRIDGES,
ZAKIYA LUNA, AND RUBY TAPIA

Just Get on the Pill

THE UNEVEN BURDEN OF
REPRODUCTIVE POLITICS

Krystale E. Littlejohn

UNIVERSITY OF CALIFORNIA PRESS

University of California Press

Oakland, California

© 2021 by Krystale E. Littlejohn

Library of Congress Cataloging-in-Publication Data

Names: Littlejohn, Krystale E., 1985– author.
Title: Just get on the pill : the uneven burden of reproductive politics /
    Krystale E. Littlejohn.
Other titles: Reproductive justice ; 4.
Description: Oakland, California : University of California Press, [2021] |
    Series: Reproductive justice : a new vision for the twenty-first
    century ; 4 | Includes bibliographical references and index.
Identifiers: LCCN 2020056074 (print) | LCCN 2020056075 (ebook) |
    ISBN 9780520307452 (paperback) | ISBN 9780520307445 (hardback) |
    ISBN 9780520973763 (ebook)
Subjects: LCSH: Human reproduction—Political aspects—United States. |
    Birth control—Political aspects—United States.
Classification: LCC HQ766.5.U6 L48 2021 (print) | LCC HQ766.5.U6
    (ebook) | DDC 363.9/60973—dc23
LC record available at https://lccn.loc.gov/2020056074
LC ebook record available at https://lccn.loc.gov/2020056075

Manufactured in the United States of America

30 29 28 27 26 25 24 23 22 21
10 9 8 7 6 5 4 3 2 1

The publisher and the University of California Press Foundation gratefully acknowledge the generous support of the Barbara S. Isgur Endowment Fund in Public Affairs.

For all people striving to live self-determined lives
amid challenge

Contents

Introduction

Sweet 16. That's how old Manuela (22 years old, Latina) was the first time she had sex with her boyfriend. They decided to take the proverbial plunge over a year into their relationship. Like many teenagers, they used condoms for birth control to start,[1] but they stopped that pretty quickly. After having sex only twice, in fact. They talked about what to do and, in Manuela's words, "We kind of thought of it together, but he kind of was the first one to say, 'I think you should just get on the pill.'" And get on the pill she did. Having a prescription for the pill made it even easier to decide what to do with her next sexual partner. They used a condom once but, unlike her experience with her boyfriend, they never talked about birth control. Instead, she said, "We just had sex and I don't know if he just assumed that I was on the pill, but we never talked about it."

Manuela's experiences with her first partners followed a similar pattern: condom use for a few encounters and the pill thereafter. No surprise there. It is often difficult for young people to consistently use condoms and not uncommon for them to switch to prescription methods like the pill at some point.[2] While Manuela had no problem relying on the pill when she first started having sex, it was only a matter of time before that division of labor stopped working for her. What happened when she decided not to "just get on the pill"? Like many people who can get pregnant, she largely struggled to use birth control after that. Though either partner can dislike condoms, Manuela's interest in condom use was not the problem. Instead, it was an inability to get her partners to use condoms as she wished. With one partner, she refused to get on the pill after he asked her to, so they had sex without birth control. And with another, "The first few months it was condom all the time, and it was a new one every single time. But, after a while he's just like, after a while no."

Experiences like Manuela's show that much more guides young people's decisions about birth control than concerns about effectiveness.[3] Her partners did not automatically default to using condoms when the prospect of pill use was off the table, even though they too wanted to avoid pregnancy. Since the invention of the pill, it has not been uncommon for people to assume that women—especially those in long-term relationships—will carry the burden of preventing pregnancy by using prescription contraception.[4] Indeed, the pill is the most widely used form of birth control in the United States, and fewer than one in ten women use two methods of contraception (e.g., condoms and the pill) simultaneously.[5] Women from groups with high rates of unintended pregnancy, defined as pregnancies that were never wanted or occurred too soon, face especially intense scrutiny of their contraceptive choices. Contraceptive use, like housework, can be considered another form of domestic labor in which women routinely engage;[6] and, like housework, ideas about gender motivate behavior.

In *Just Get on the Pill*, I explore how gendered assumptions and expectations shape women's birth control experiences with their partners. The book is grounded in the stories of women like

Angelica (a pseudonym), who told me when it came to preventing pregnancy with her boyfriend, "I think he kind of just left it up to me to make sure that I'm grown and I need to take care of it. I think that was his mentality, like well, you're a woman, you're grown, handle your business type thing." Angelica did "handle her business"—by using prescription birth control—without complaint. Her inability to use her method consistently and her boyfriend's resistance to using condoms, however, resulted in a pregnancy. Angelica's narrative, and those of over a hundred other women, showed me how the division of labor in birth control plays out in women's lives. I argue that gender inequality in birth control use is not the result of either natural differences between male and female bodies or incidental differences in the effectiveness of "men's" versus "women's" methods. Women like Angelica are not left to shoulder the burden of preventing pregnancy without help from their partners simply because the birth control methods "designed for" women's bodies are more effective. Indeed, prescription birth control is quite ineffective for women who dislike it, lack regular access to it, or prefer not to use it. Instead, I show that parents, peers, partners, and providers socialize women into using "female" birth control methods and ultimately into accepting primary responsibility for preventing pregnancy—a phenomenon I call *gendered compulsory birth control*.

Just Get on the Pill demonstrates that gendered compulsory birth control has a number of overlooked, but nonetheless severe, consequences—namely, it undermines women's rights by reducing their control over their bodies, eroding their reproductive autonomy, and constraining their ability to have sex safely and without coercion. Using an intersectional lens, I show how Black and less advantaged women adopted novel approaches to the compulsory birth control system, especially by refusing to begin prescription birth control when partners will not wear condoms. Nevertheless, researchers may sometimes inadvertently recast these women's strategies in the power-neutral language of *contraceptive inconsistency* or *nonuse* because the dominant family planning approach in the United States positions prescription birth control for women as the solution to unintended pregnancy. I show that compelling the use of prescription birth control as the sole "woman's method," especially when partners refuse to use condoms, ultimately harms women by making it more difficult for them to protect themselves from disease. Counterintuitively, it can also complicate pregnancy prevention because most women are channeled away from buying, carrying, and using condoms (a "man's method"), even if they have trouble using the methods assigned to them. In the end, I show that the gendered organization of birth control is not natural. It is unjust.

INEQUALITY IN THE PREGNANCY PREVENTION PRESCRIPTION

Although battles over the power to regulate women's reproductive experiences have a long history in the United States,[7] contraceptive behavior became the subject of regular public study only in the first part of the twentieth century. The American Medical Association declared contraception a medical issue in 1937, on the grounds that "the intelligent, voluntary spacing of pregnancies may be desirable for the health and general well-being of mothers and children."[8] This declaration gave physicians the authority to discuss contraception with their patients. The first study to examine people's pregnancy attitudes and behaviors was conducted just a few years later in 1941, when the Indianapolis study surveyed almost fifteen hundred couples about their pregnancy attitudes and contraceptive behavior.[9] While the study sought to understand how to *increase* the fertility of married, white, Protestant women (because of eugenic fears about the falling birth rate for this group), demographers and public health experts later focused their attention on eugenic efforts to *decrease* population growth for groups whose fertility they categorized as "undesirable."[10] These attempts included contraception and sterilization campaigns aimed at eradicating the fertility of people of color, the poor, and the mentally ill.[11] The Indianapolis study introduced the idea of unintended pregnancy and put women's fertility intentions on the map as a public health issue.[12] Even at this early date, women were the focus of efforts concerning pregnancy prevention.

The establishment of a field of study dedicated to women's fertility and women's pregnancy intentions supported efforts to monitor women's reproductive experiences long after overt eugenic campaigns had faded. Since its publication in 1995, *The Best Intentions: Unintended Pregnancy and the Well-Being of Children and Families,* a book published by the Institute of Medicine, has been one of the most important publications to direct the agenda for research on pregnancy and childbirth.[13] The book opens by noting that nearly 60 percent of pregnancies in the United States at the time were mistimed or unwanted. The authors then argue that to reduce the incidence of unintended pregnancy, the United States must reformulate its cultural approach by establishing "a new consensus that pregnancy needs to be undertaken only with clear intent."[14] Every pregnancy, in other words, should be *planned* for every person. The committee notes that this goal "is directed at all Americans" and "emphasizes personal choice and intent."[15] Increasing contraceptive access, knowledge, and use were positioned as central to helping people plan pregnancies, thereby reducing the number of unintended conceptions and abortions. The book did not contend with how focusing on planning and preventing pregnancy as the ultimate goal could have disproportionate consequences for women in general, and marginalized women in particular. Inequity in today's pregnancy prevention frameworks and strategies can be traced back, at least in part, to the recommendations in this book and the overlooked consequences of its arguments.

In the years since the publication of *The Best Intentions,* the percentage of conceptions labeled as unintended has remained high (e.g., 45 percent in 2011), and public health experts have doubled down on efforts to convince couples to use contraceptives during every sexual encounter.[16] While both partners contribute to conception, research on unintended pregnancy usually focuses on cisgender women. Of all unintended pregnancies that did not result in miscarriages in 2011, just over 40 percent resulted in a birth and nearly 60 percent resulted in an abortion.[17] Dissecting these data reveals that young women, women of color, and women who are poor or have low incomes are most likely to have an unintended pregnancy.[18] In addition, Black women and those with low incomes are more likely than women from other racial and class groups to have an abortion. Researchers note that while the nearly 70 percent of women who use contraceptives consistently and correctly account for only a very small fraction of unintended pregnancies (5 percent), the roughly 30 percent of women who do not use contraceptives, or use them inconsistently, account for 95 percent of all unintended pregnancies.[19] This focus on women ignores their partners as equal participants in sex and conception, de-emphasizing their actions in preventing or contributing to unintended pregnancy. Instead, many researchers and clinicians consider family planning for the person with a uterus to be central to preventing pregnancy for couples.

From a public health perspective, scholars and policy makers view ensuring that each pregnancy is planned as not only a personal goal that cisgender women should strive for but also as a social imperative crucial to cutting economic costs and improving a variety of health outcomes.[20] As historian Rickie Solinger noted, the management of women's fertility has often been advanced as a tool for solving a variety of social problems, even as women's bodies and best interests are subordinated to a discussion of what regulating their bodies might accomplish.[21] In the case of unintended pregnancy, getting women to "plan their pregnancies" and reduce unintended births have been championed as important contributors to reducing poverty, improving childhood outcomes, and reducing rates of poor mental health (due to having children from an unintended conception).[22] In *Healthy People 2020*—a set of public health goals set by the Centers for Disease Control and Prevention every decade—family planning is portrayed as important because reducing unintended pregnancies saves the government money, and family planning clinics serve large swaths of women.[23] Thus, at both the individual and national levels, managing women's fertility is upheld as the cure for a multitude of public health concerns. *Just Get on the Pill* reveals the significant negative consequences of this approach for women's control over their bodies.

Campaigns to reduce unintended pregnancy overwhelmingly focus on cisgender women, often without acknowledging how this focus affects contraceptive use in their relationships and sexual encounters. In the presidential address at the Annual Clinical Meeting of the American College of Obstetricians and Gynecologists in 1999, for example, Dr. Frank C. Miller asserted,

"Contraception must be made available to teens who are sexually active, especially to adolescent girls for the prevention of unintended pregnancies as well as deadly STDs."[24] He implored clinicians to become leaders in their communities because "these are our sisters and our daughters, and they deserve better. They need our help."[25] Reflecting Dr. Miller's focus on the central role of women and girls in the discussion of birth control, contraceptive counseling guidelines state that while providers should discuss all methods with patients, they should discuss those considered particularly effective (i.e., prescription methods requiring women to visit medical providers) first.[26] Notably, even a 2014 policy statement on adolescent contraception released by the American Academy of Pediatrics suggested that providers begin by discussing the most effective contraceptive methods (which offer no protection from sexually transmitted infections [STIs]), even though adolescents and young adults accounted for 66 percent of all reported chlamydia cases at the time.[27] Some researchers have taken recommendations to prioritize effective contraception one step further by issuing calls for women to use prescription birth control that is effective for several years to reduce the "burden of unintended pregnancy."[28] With the rise of prepregnancy care, which focuses primarily on individual women,[29] the gendered surveillance of women's bodies will likely remain unchanged for the foreseeable future.

Perhaps because of the overwhelming focus on women in family planning, their partners have trouble accessing information on birth control. Many clinics have programs only for women, and, even when men do interact with health care providers, they are less likely than women to receive information on birth control methods.[30] This is particularly problematic because over 75 percent of men have become sexually active by age 20.[31] Thus, while both men and women contribute to conception in heterosexual encounters, men do not experience the same pressures to "manage" their fertility. This fact is not lost on ordinary women. A young woman whom I call Jennifer, for example, wished there were "men's birth control" because pregnancy prevention "is sort of all up to me." Isabella also noted the unfairness of the birth control playing field, asserting "I think that it's also the guy's job too to have other methods. I don't understand, like there's all this research that goes into finding easier ways to implant things for women and things like that but there's not that much that goes into easier ways for men too. Because a lot of men find condoms a hassle."

Even as several social factors contribute to women's assuming primary responsibility for preventing pregnancy and birth, observers not uncommonly explain this inequality by citing "the reality" that the most highly effective methods of contraception are designed for women.[32] Such explanations assume that differences in the effectiveness of "men's" and "women's" birth control methods drive contraceptive behavior—an assumption predicated on first categorizing birth control according to people's bodies. From the notion that birth control methods with different levels of effectiveness are made for differently sexed bodies to the notion that cisgender women are responsible for preventing pregnancy because they bear children, unexamined assumptions about gender enjoy unmerited prominence in both popular and academic explanations for the gendered division of labor in birth control. Even justifications premised on clearly faulty logic, such as the belief that interventions target women because a single man can impregnate many women, abound. All of these explanations rest on biological determinism (the idea that biology explains behavior), which researchers have vociferously refuted in other domains.

Interrogating the veracity of such explanations is one of the central tasks of this book.

IMAGINING REPRODUCTIVE JUSTICE

Understanding women's experiences with birth control requires moving beyond thinking about individual women to thinking about the social world that enables and constrains their behaviors. In *Just Get on the Pill*, I analyze women's experiences using a quality of mind that considers the connection between a person's individual situation, the historical moment, and the workings of important institutions like families that make up society. This frame of mind—called the sociological imagination—pushes us to understand that individuals reside within a larger cultural and historical context.[33] From this perspective, women's reproductive experiences cannot be examined in isolation from the larger cultural, historical, medical, and legal forces that act on and through their bodies. I grapple with how social factors mediate the relationship between the meanings of women's fertility and the dominant public health frameworks for determining the best way to manage births. In *Just Get on the Pill*, I show that gender is central to this task and, with regard to the bodies of women, gender goes hand in hand with race and class.

In analyzing gender, I draw on social constructionism, which posits that social categories do not have inherent meaning, but rather acquire it as people come together to define and create meaning through social interaction. One of the key contributions feminist theorists have made to social science is the idea that sex and gender are not equivalent. *People* create and enact ideas about sexed bodies, and those understandings and behaviors help define what is called gender.[34] In this sense, biological sex refers to the categorization of people as "male," "female," or "intersex" (among others) at birth, and gender encompasses the ideas created and behaviors enacted because of beliefs about difference. I argue that it is insufficient to assert simply that gender is mapped onto male and female bodies. Instead, I am interested in examining *how* gender comes about. If sex and gender are different, how do gendered understandings and behaviors emerge from sexed bodies? Further, what are the consequences of these understandings? Birth control use, with its typical focus on male and female bodies in both the larger discourse on contraception and in people's daily lives, presents an ideal site for uncovering how gender operates. In examining these processes, I reveal how contemporary approaches to birth control violate women's right to reproductive justice.

Reproductive justice is a framework and movement that holds "it is important to fight equally for (1) the right to have a child, (2) the right not to have a child, and (3) the right to parent the children we have."[35] A group of Black women activists first coined the term in 1994. The SisterSong Women of Color Reproductive Health Collective, a group of sixteen organizations of women of color that emphasizes public policy and mobilization at the grassroots level, promoted the use of the term within a human rights framework.[36] Within a few years of its establishment in 1997, the collective grew to eighty organizations.[37] Cofounding member of SisterSong Loretta Ross noted that reproductive justice unites reproductive rights and social justice.[38] Advocates advance reproductive justice as a framework that better addresses the variety of threats that women of color and marginalized women face in their daily lives, arguing that the mainstream reproductive rights movement focuses too narrowly on the individual right to abortion and "choice" as the chief issues of concern.[39]

Proponents of reproductive justice argue that because some women's fertility is valued and policed more than other women's—what scholars refer to as *stratified reproduction*—truly protecting their bodies and lives requires a more expansive framework.[40] This framework must account for differences in societal responses to women's fertility based on their social location, as well as the ways that women's reproductive freedom depends on their race, gender, class, immigration status, and other axes of power. As sociologists and legal scholars Zakiya Luna and Kristin Luker noted, using a reproductive justice framework expands the focus beyond abortion to "include a broader range of settings and practices in which inequalities of class, race, and gender are re-created in and on the bodies of women and their communities."[41]

In addition to emphasizing the human right to have a child, the human right not to have a child, and the human right to parent in safe and healthy environments, reproductive justice also emphasizes sexual rights and sexual citizenship.[42] In 1995, at the Fourth UN World Conference on Women in Beijing, the Platform for Action adopted by the conference made a strong statement on women's sexual rights:

> The human rights of women include their right to have control over and decide freely and responsibly on matters related to their sexuality, including sexual and reproductive health, free of coercion, discrimination and violence. Equal relationships between women and men in matters of sexual relations and reproduction, including full respect for the integrity of the person, require mutual respect, consent and shared responsibility for sexual behaviour and its consequences.[43]

Women, therefore, have the fundamental human right *not* to shoulder the burden of exclusive responsibility for preventing pregnancy. The focus on the right to dignity, shared responsibility, and intersectionality makes reproductive justice a particularly powerful framework for uncovering how everyday social practices reinscribe gender as a legitimate basis for inequality.

Reproductive justice positions eradicating reproductive oppression as fundamental to ensuring women's reproductive freedom. Asian Communities for Reproductive Justice (now Forward Together), a founding member of the SisterSong Women of Color Reproductive Health Collective, defined reproductive oppression as "the controlling and exploiting of women and girls through our bodies, sexuality, and reproduction (both biological and social) by families, communities, institutions, and societies."[44] Reproductive justice stresses the idea that whether the issue is contraception, abortion, or parenthood, oppression is not about anatomy but rather is a matter of power and relationships of power.[45] Reproductive justice centers and contextualizes the needs, rights, and health of women, who are impacted by efforts to manage their fertility via societal-level emphases on population control or individual-level emphases on the desires of their partners and families. Reproductive oppression becomes particularly concerning as governments and policy makers consistently return to women's bodies to resolve social problems and define some women's bodies as "risky."[46] In the case of unintended pregnancy, all sexually active women are considered "at risk," especially women of color and poor women because they belong to groups with higher rates of unintended pregnancy. Reproductive justice is a particularly useful framework for studying reproductive oppression because it applies to all women, both privileged and not, even as it draws attention to the disproportionate consequences of fertility control efforts for women of color.[47]

In *Just Get on the Pill*, I reveal a type of reproductive injustice—what I view as an inequity in sexual and reproductive health, autonomy, or (in)fertility resulting from the unequal social patterning, deployment, and distribution of resources (broadly defined). I argue that the gendered division of labor and women's primary responsibility for preventing births are not reflections of inevitable inequality based on biological difference. Rather, the suggestion that widespread inequity can be explained by differences in bodies and the effectiveness of methods is premised on unquestioned assumptions about gender and a historically and culturally decontextualized treatment of reproduction. This framework for understanding reproduction treats women's experiences with unintended pregnancy and STIs as the results of individual failures to use birth control when they do not desire a pregnancy or to use condoms when a partner's health status is unclear. This perspective precludes an analysis of how women navigate and resist larger cultural frameworks about fertility that intersect with race, gender, and class. Most of all, divorcing pregnancy prevention from social context legitimates the argument that women take full responsibility for preventing pregnancy because they birth children, rather than because their behavior is culturally variable, socially influenced, and historically specific.

In *Just Get on the Pill*, I share the experiences of over a hundred diverse women from the San Francisco Bay Area, whose stories I learned about when I was part of a research team that conducted interviews from 2009 to 2011. I use pseudonyms to protect their identities. The women, all unmarried and between the ages of 20 and 29, were recruited from two community colleges and two four-year universities to gather a broad swath of perspectives across socioeconomic status. By design, approximately half of the women had experienced a pregnancy while the other half had not. I provide more detail on the sample in the appendix. In *Just Get on the Pill*, I examine these women's experiences with birth control as an intersectional gendered social process, recognizing that women have long had to contend with social efforts to regulate their fertility and have long developed unique responses that can reveal not what some women are doing right but what social policies are doing wrong. In the interviews, we asked women to tell us about their sexual encounters; their experiences with contraception, pregnancy, and abortion; and their goals for the future. The stories that these young women told taught me a great deal about how social approaches to birth control both helped and hindered their efforts to create self-determined lives. Learning lessons from their narratives required three elements: my willingness to challenge core cultural values and assumptions; women participants who were brave and generous enough to recount the truth of their experiences, even when their behaviors result in stigma and shame; and a Black feminist way of knowing that centers the validity of all women's stories for the creation of knowledge.[48] I worked hard to achieve and deploy all three.

In *Just Get on the Pill*, I argue that the gendered compulsory birth control system, which emphasizes birth control use only for women, exploits women's bodies as well as their labor. Indeed, only in the context of the gendered exploitation of women's bodies can the work women do to help millions of men prevent pregnancy every year be cast as natural, and indeed beneficial, *only* for women. The analysis shows how a focus on privileging choice around prescription birth control and abortion masks the ways that gendered understandings of birth control can harm women. In addition to portraying the behavior of those who resist the system (by stopping or never taking prescription contraceptives) as undisciplined, it casts all women who become pregnant under "nonideal" circumstances as culpable for a host of social problems that their adoption of gendered frameworks in birth control will not solve.

STRUCTURE OF THE BOOK

In chapter 1, I show how women often categorized condoms as a "man's method." In this framework, condoms are for men and methods that interact with female bodies (e.g., pills, the diaphragm) are for women. This categorization aligns with dominant understandings of these birth control methods in medicine and public health. Using a sociological lens, I show that the belief that (external) condoms are for men stems from gendered understandings of bodies rather than from natural differences. Indeed, because condoms come into contact with both partners' bodies and provide visible protection from STIs and pregnancy for both partners, it is not a given that they must be understood as only a "man's method." Nonetheless, I show how the understanding that condoms are "his thing" directed otherwise sexually comfortable women away from buying, bringing, and handling condoms. In fact, as Olivia (whom I discuss in the next chapter) mentions, she rarely worried about condoms because she believed "it's the guy's responsibility to go to the store and buy one, you know."

Chapter 2 focuses on how women prioritized using prescription birth control and other methods that interact with female bodies (e.g., the diaphragm) as appropriate "women's methods." I show that women's decisions to prioritize prescription birth control cannot be explained simply by citing strong motivations to prevent pregnancy (manifested in the use of the most effective methods) because these same women also had sex without condoms, even when they were using prescription birth control methods inconsistently, or before the methods became effective. Importantly, I show that women remained resilient in trying to find a prescription birth control method that worked for them despite widespread dissatisfaction.

In Chapter 3, I introduce the concept of gendered compulsory birth control. I show how partners, parents, and medical providers encouraged women to assume primary responsibility for preventing births using prescription birth control. This pattern not only exposed women to greater risks of contracting STIs but also disempowered some women, who either preferred or were better suited for "male" methods, such as condoms. I describe how in the most extreme cases—instances in which partners removed condoms during sex without the woman's knowledge—women were literally compelled to use prescription methods, such as emergency contraception, even when they preferred to avoid hormonal methods altogether. Finally, I illustrate how women's choices about how to resolve a pregnancy were constrained when they failed at their gendered duty to "do their part" in preventing pregnancy.

Chapter 4 elucidates how some women resisted typical expectations of gendered behavior in birth control use. These women, largely Black and less advantaged, often refused to start using prescription birth control methods if their partners would not cooperate with wearing condoms and often did not transition from using condoms early in the relationship to exclusively using prescription methods when the relationship became more serious. These women's refusal to use prescription birth control sometimes resulted in their not using *any* form of birth control if they had partners who refused to use condoms. Although this choice made them more susceptible to pregnancy, the chapter shows their actions were not poorly considered "contraceptive mistakes" but rather stemmed from a conscious decision to avoid giving in to their partners' unfair expectations.

In the final pages of the book, I discuss both the implications of the findings for contemporary approaches to pregnancy prevention in the United States and the harm that decontextualized approaches cause women. I illustrate the value of "gendered compulsory birth control" and "reproductive (in)justice" as concepts by showing how the analysis debunks the "commonsense" assumptions that gender inequality in birth control is natural and prescription birth control use is *always* beneficial for all women. Instead, *Just Get on the Pill* demonstrates the crucial need to center women's reproductive autonomy by asking, not *whether* the pill benefits women, but rather *under what conditions* it does so.

1   *His Condom*

You know, I don't really remember there being very much sexual education. Like I never took health because I think I opted out of it. I forget what I took instead. No, I took health online. There wasn't really much talk about it in my family. It was weird. I never got the birds and the bees conversation, like I used to read romance books but they never talked about birth control. Never. No one would be like, "And he put his condom on."

AUDREY, 20 years old, white

Although many girls like Audrey never get the "birds and the bees" talk, they learn their ideas about condoms from somewhere. Research exploring the meaning of condoms shows that women may hesitate to ask partners to use condoms because they fear it signals a lack of trust or indicates that the woman herself is unfaithful.[1] We know very little about nonrelationship contraceptive meanings, despite the fact that sex outside of "committed" relationships is more common today than in years past.[2] These more casual contexts are the very ones in which people are most likely to use condoms.[3] Thus, how do women think about condoms? And how do these understandings shape how they use them with their partners? In this chapter, as in the rest of this book, I argue that gender plays a central role.

People are socialized into gendered bodies at young ages,[4] and social framings of birth control serve as one more tool to teach people how to think about their bodies and behavior. Teaching people to behave according to standards expected of their gender (gender socialization) includes communicating expectations that girls should be moral and chaste,[5] boys should seek sex for pleasure and status,[6] and young girls should be especially careful to avoid pregnancy.[7] Through gender socialization, girls also learn they must act as sexual "gatekeepers."[8] These are more or less well-known gender norms dictating what people should and should not do sexually. In this chapter, I argue that these norms coexist alongside taken-for-granted ideas about how *genders* should protect themselves sexually. As condoms come into contact with both partners' genitals and protect them both from pregnancies and sexually transmitted infections (STIs), it is theoretically possible to think of condoms without invoking gendered ideas about difference. I show that in practice, however, condoms are separated into versions for "males" and "females," and these ideas have important consequences for behavior.

Public health campaigns aimed at reducing teen and "unplanned" pregnancy play an important role in both reflecting and shaping ideas about birth control. Despite efforts to get *couples* to use condoms during penile-vaginal intercourse, the broader discourse in medicine and public health communicates the very gendered message that some condoms are for men and some are for women. Take the most widely used graphic on the effectiveness of different birth control methods, for example. One such chart is linked on the Centers for Disease Control and Prevention's "Contraception" page. The chart clearly labels condoms worn externally as "male condoms" and those worn internally as "female condoms."[9] People looking up information about birth control online are unlikely to be enthralled by a more technical chart on the effectiveness of different methods. They may, however, read other information that the CDC posts to encourage "safe sex." The message they receive there is not any less gendered. Indeed, perusing the contraception page leads to a "His Condom + Her Birth Control" infographic used to encourage people to use two methods of birth control (a condom plus a prescription method).[10] Both a policy statement released by the American Academy of Pediatrics[11] and a committee opinion released by the American College of Obstetricians and Gynecologists[12] also explicitly refer to the "male condom." These are only a few examples. Gendered messages linking particular condoms to particular bodies are widespread in public health.

Thinking of condoms in this way may seem both natural and unproblematic. I argue that it is neither. Condoms need not be tied to the gendered bodies that people presume will use them. Women having sex with women can use male condoms and men having sex with men can use female condoms. In fact, research shows not only that some men having sex with men already use the female condom with their partners but also that some of them actually prefer it over the male condom.[13] Thinking of condoms as "male" and "female," therefore, has less to do with biological necessity than with social thinking about bodies and heterosexuality. Not only does this framing leave trans and intersex people's experiences out of the conversation but it also suggests that the condoms that men wear are *by definition* out of women's control—that is, men are the "implied user," as feminist scholars have articulated in other domains.[14] In this way, the social framing of contraception plays an important role in reinforcing gendered expectations of heterosexual behavior by encouraging women to center men's desires in condom use.[15] *Just Get on the Pill* extends work in this tradition by examining pregnancy prevention as a site where heterosexuality and gender operate as social structures that sustain inequity but do not receive widespread critique because biological determinism dominates explanations of inequality. I show that social ideas about to whom condoms "belong" matter tremendously for decision-making autonomy in contraception.

Messages that "condom" is synonymous with "man" coexist with strategies to change that messaging, even if only to get women to buy condoms. Ironically, the marketing strategies aimed at changing women's behavior only further underscore the entrenchment of gendered ideas about birth control in US society. Trojan, "America's Leading Condom Brand," for example, introduced a condom line just for women in 2017. Its name? The XOXO condom—a condom that is no different functionally than its regular Trojan condom. The XOXO condom simply has "Softouch thin latex and aloe-infused lubricant," with packaging (lavender) that "is designed to be discreet, so [women] can carry it as confidently as [they] carry [themselves]."[16] The vice president of marketing emphasized that the new line reflected a viewpoint positing that "it's not just like, 'Hey, I'm the guy, I bring the condom.'" Instead, the company had to introduce a condom line for women because "[Trojan] did not want to make this pink-washed. . . . This [the external condom] is not a girl's condom."[17] Indeed, regardless of new marketing strategies, women are taught that it is a man's.

In this chapter, I show how larger cultural messages like those just described reflect on-the-ground thinking about birth control. I argue that women associate external condoms with men's bodies and men's actions, and they feel much less comfortable bringing, buying, and interacting with condoms as a result. These messages are both communicated and reinforced by families, friends, sexual partners, and health professionals. Indeed, this chapter shows that the gender-based assumption that external condoms are for men (largely because they are *worn* by them) is pervasive.

"THEY SEPARATED THE GIRLS AND THE BOYS AND TAUGHT THEM DIFFERENT LESSONS"

Compared with the more explicit gender-based messaging that teen girls might receive from sex education (like avoiding promiscuity),[18] gendered messaging around birth control appeared to be more subtle in women's discussions. Most women who had taken sex education discussed learning about both condoms and "the pill." Few recalled explicit details about exactly how educators framed the methods. Their descriptions demonstrated nonetheless how sex education could normalize gendered logics around birth control—sometimes even before students were actually having sex. Miranda (28 years old, white) recalled how she first learned about contraception:

> I think from like, what do they call those classes in elementary school? Like "Family Life" or something like that. They had some really funny name for them. That's the first time I remember hearing about it was like, fifth or sixth grade . . . . I remember that they separated the girls and boys and they taught them different lessons, but I remember that everybody talked about it afterward and like, swapped stories. So yeah, I generally remember what they said. It was pretty basic.

Whether her school "separated the girls and boys" because of maturity concerns over teaching young people about sex, or because they actually intended to teach separate lessons, as Miranda contended, the notion that the sexes are intrinsically different is a central component of gender ideology.[19] Separating girls and boys during sex education helps establish the gendered expectation that different bodies necessarily need different birth control. In fact, for women like Olivia (26 years old, Asian), sex education included learning to use explicitly sexed technologies, such as "how to use different kind[s] of condoms, female condoms, male condoms, [and] pills."

It might be argued that, while it is certainly gendered, framing condoms as "male" and "female" matters less for *gender inequality* because women at least have the internal condom as their own. Even when bracketing my contention that marketing different condoms to different genders is harmful, this thinking is flawed—namely, because the internal condom is more expensive than the external one and use is low around the globe.[20] Though a minority of women in this study mentioned internal condoms, very few of them had used them. Isis (21 years old, Black) was one of the few women who even expressed interest in doing so. Her mother had talked with her about "the female condom," the ring, and spermicide ("as another method that women can use"). In a portion of the interview, in which she discussed what her mom had told her about birth control, Isis mentioned "the female condom" and said simply that "I've never used it but I think I might want to try or figure it out." That was the extent of the conversation. Indeed, internal condom use seemed to be an afterthought for most women, if it was even considered an option at all.

External condom use was a much more popular topic of conversation, but parents did little to facilitate women's use with their partners, even when they supported the behavior. With respect to parents as potential facilitators of contraceptive access, what they did mattered more than what they said. And what they did usually encouraged young women to conform to gendered norms around birth control, wherein they abdicated responsibility for condoms. Parents, for example, might tell their daughters to use condoms but not do anything to help them. Instead, they focused much more on getting their daughters prescription birth control. In recalling her experience learning about contraception, Molly (20 years old, white) said, "We had the fifth-grade talk about your body changing, and I'm sure at some point we had this sex ed. talk because I seem to recall one. Although maybe not. Maybe my mom was like, 'You should use a condom if you have sex.' I don't know." Although Molly believed that her mom encouraged condom use, that support did not translate into financial help. Molly had the following conversation with the interviewer:

MOLLY: [My boyfriend] bought the condoms. So I never did that and I never asked my mom. But with [prescription] birth control, she was all for it. My dad knows I'm on birth control. I mean also because it really was at first for my cramps. It's not like my mom didn't know I was having sex because she definitely did. I never brought it up with my dad but my mom is totally cool with it. She pays for it and everything.

INTERVIEWER: So your mom knew that you were having sex?

MOLLY: Yes, I told her.

INTERVIEWER: How did that conversation go?

MOLLY: She was mad at [him]. She was like, "I thought he was a good Christian boy and you were gonna wait until you were married." But then she got over it pretty quickly.

Thus, while Molly's mom may have told her to use condoms, she never actually followed up to make sure Molly had access to them.

Instead, her mom focused on supporting Molly's use of a prescription birth control method. I return to parents' role in facilitating girls' prescription birth control use in the next chapter. The point here is to demonstrate how parents' lack of financial support for condoms could reify the message that girls need not worry about condom provision itself, even when parents were supportive of their daughters using the method.

Interestingly, while fathers did not usually discuss *any* method of birth control with their daughters, they almost always discussed condoms when the topic came up. This may be surprising if one considers only gendered messaging about condoms and sexual promiscuity for girls but not if one considers the broader gendering of birth control methods that I articulate in this book. In this framework, it makes sense that fathers would teach daughters about condoms because they themselves were unlikely to be taught about other methods. Trisha (22 years old, Black) talked about how her family handled conversations about contraception:

> My mom never said anything. It was one of those things that was like my dad always took control of those type of situations. My parents were the ones that will be like, "just don't have sex." It was never like, "here, let me educate you about sex and how to have it safely if you decide." It was more like, "don't have sex or I'll kill you." It was like that. It was like they just told me not to do it. So, they never really took the time to talk to me about those different types of things other than my dad saying if I ever decide to have sex make sure that we use a condom.

While Trisha received "mixed messages" about sex and contraception (that is, "don't have sex, but use condoms if you do"),[21] she picked up on the message that helping her have safe sex was a low priority for her family. Like Molly, her parents never helped her strategize about condoms (or any other form of birth control) when she started having sex, but they did help her strategize during her pregnancy when she conceived at 17.

Facilitating girls' access to condoms might have appeared less important to parents because women are not the implied users. But because men *are,* their satisfaction with condoms could play an important role in determining whether women in the study saw condoms as a viable protection strategy. When discussing frequent unprotected sex (that is, not using any contraception regardless of method effectiveness) with her current partner, Audrey (20 years old, white) said the following:

> INTERVIEWER: Did you ever have any conversations or conflicts about using protection? Like maybe someone not wanting to and the other person wanting to?
>
> AUDREY: With anybody or with him?
>
> INTERVIEWER: Him.
>
> AUDREY: Well, the thing is, I don't know if it's the case with other guys, but I guess having a condom can be difficult for a guy sometime. I mean I guess it is just a plastic bag. Let's be honest here. It's like Saran Wrap. Who the hell invented a condom? They must have been tortured here. I don't know. I know it's difficult for that.

What is interesting about Audrey is that she *preferred* using the condom and had no problem using a condom every time she had sex with her previous partner. That relationship lasted over a year. Yet she framed condoms as a "torture" device because her current boyfriend said he could not maintain an erection while wearing one. In recalling how she and her partner figured out what they would do for birth control if they didn't use condoms, her partner asserted that they "just won't do it protected." Audrey's partner's preferences, therefore, dominated the couple's decision to have unprotected sex, and his dissatisfaction overwhelmingly shaped her framing of condoms as a bad method for "guys" even though she preferred it as a "girl." That a latex barrier reduced friction and skin-to-skin contact for *her*, in fact, escaped her notice altogether when she defined condoms as akin to a torturous "plastic bag," and she still felt satisfied using the method.

Even when men's dissatisfaction was not at issue, how they framed condom use could nonetheless contribute to understandings that men themselves were the implied users. Carolina (26 years old, Latina) recalled her partner centering himself in order to assuage her fears about having sex for the first time. When discussing which of them initiated conversations about birth control with her first partner, she said, "I think he did just because, you know, trying to convince me or talk about it, you know, 'If we do [have sex], I'll always be safe about it [wearing a condom], and there's never gonna be'—trying to avoid the consequences of me getting pregnant." Carolina's boyfriend thus saw himself as the primary user of the condom, even though his goal was to convince her she did not have to worry about getting pregnant because *they* would use a condom. Carolina's own ideas about contraception, however, made his argument less convincing. For her, pregnancy happens "when you're ready or it happens because it's gonna happen" —that is, regardless of whether a couple uses contraception. When talking about her boyfriend's orientation toward sex and pregnancy, Carolina said, "He was worried, he's like 'I'm not ready to have a kid so if we do, you know,' just the fact that he wasn't—he was ready to do the act but not ready to ever have any consequences for it." For him, that meant promising her that *he* would always be safe by wearing a condom.

The way that some women talked about condoms suggested that larger gendered frameworks shaped even understandings of who actually used the method during intercourse. Their comments echoed Carolina's boyfriend's assertion that men, not the couple, used the condom. Nearly 40 percent of women in the interviews discussed condoms that men wear in ways that explicitly linked condoms only to men's bodies and men's actions, despite the fact that condoms come into contact with both partners' genitals during intercourse.[22] Women did this even when they provided the condom. The "(external) condom" became the "man's condom" in ways that were largely unnoticed and unproblematic to many women (and, according to women's narratives, their partners). Holly (20 years old, white), for example, fought with her long-term boyfriend when she decided to stop the pill because it meant they had to return to using condoms. When discussing the experience, Holly said, "[My boyfriend] wanted me to stay on the pill more and I think that was the only time we ever had a conflict. I think that he liked that *he* didn't have to use a condom every time. But I kind of just did my own thing 'cause I figured at the end of the day, it's my body, so he can kiss my butt" (emphasis added). Interestingly, Holly associated the pill (not the condom) with her right to control her body—even though they would be using condoms to protect her from pregnancy. She asserted her bodily autonomy to explain why she could easily ignore her boyfriend's assertions that she stay on the *pill* (a "woman's method").

Even when women explicitly communicated their interest in protecting themselves from STIs, they did in some cases still use language that undermined their role as simultaneous condom users. Sharon (24 years old, Black), for example, talked about how she always used both condoms and the pill with an ex-boyfriend. In discussing conversations with her boyfriend about condoms, she told the interviewer that she would say, "I don't trust you. I am making you use a rubber, so fuck off." Thinking of using a condom as something that the man *does,* rather than something that he *wears,* was not limited to relationships with low trust. Were condoms not already associated with bodies, one could imagine Sharon telling her partner that she was making *them* use a condom, which in fact is what *they* were doing. In making her boyfriend wear a condom, Sharon protected herself from both pregnancy and disease. The form of protection just so happened to be worn on her partner's penis. Positioning the sex of "the wearer" as the primary factor in determining whose method it is (i.e., internal or external condom) makes sense only in a context in which gendered meanings already proliferate. In this sense, condoms are no less gendered than pants, dresses, or shoes. Though gender scholars focus less on contraception as a gendered social process, I argue that the idea that a particular condom belongs to a particular gender is social not natural.

Some women's narratives suggested that social power played a role in their understandings of condoms as a man's method. When discussing the conversations about birth control that she had with an ex-boyfriend, Enola (21 years old, American Indian) said, "He wanted me to get an intrauterine device, yeah. IUD. And because, I'm not even sure why. We had been talking about how hormones can be fucking me up, birth control, stuff like that." When the interviewer asked about any issues with condoms or the pill, Enola mentioned, "[my ex-boyfriend] was shady about using *his* condoms sometimes" (emphasis added). Later, she revealed why she felt that way: "So on one of the occasions, my ex-boyfriend came to visit and like we were technically broken up and I felt sorry for him and let him stay. And that situation, he had used a condom but didn't use a condom, like he messed it up and it got lost inside of me." In response to her ex-boyfriend saying, "Oh, crap. I lost the condom," she took Plan B, which she always kept on hand "just in case." It may have been reasonable for Enola to understand the condom as "his" given her skepticism that "he messed it up" unintentionally. Because he took away her control of the condom, in other words, she may not have felt like it was hers. I would argue that gendered power is not the only reason that Enola talked about her ex-boyfriend being shady about using "his" condoms. As a thought experiment, one need only consider a parallel situation involving a female condom. If Enola's ex-boyfriend had removed the internal condom from her vagina, for example, would she still believe that *he* was shady about using *his* condoms? Or would she be more inclined to understand his behavior as removing *her* condom, *the* condom, or the *female* condom?

Given that I have focused on the social tendency to center men in social framings of the external condom, I would be remiss if I failed to discuss how women actually felt about them. As one might imagine, not all women felt satisfied with condoms and a minority had serious concerns. Amanda (21 years old, white), for example, said, "Personally, I don't really like condoms. I think they're weird and gross so I would prefer to just use [prescription] birth control. But I've had such ups and downs with it [prescription birth control], not in the sense of pregnancy, but more in the sense of how it made me feel. I don't know how I feel about it so I'm going to keep trying until I feel like I'm comfortable with birth control." When the interviewer asked her what she disliked about condoms,

Amanda said, "They're just weird. I don't like the feel of them. I don't like the idea that it's a foreign object, whatever it's made of, latex or whatever. It just kinda irks me to think of that." While it was simply the nature of condoms that bothered Amanda, other women like Deborah (20 years old, white) and Rachel (26 years old, white) disliked condoms because they felt that it made sex less pleasurable. As public health researchers Jenny Higgins and Jennifer Hirsch found, both men and women care deeply about using methods that maximize pleasure and decrease discomfort.[23] Deborah was unique in being one of the few women in the study who primarily used withdrawal at the time of the interview because "for [me], sex feels better without a condom." Rachel, on the other hand, said, "Well, I, me, personally I don't like condoms because it irritates me. I'll use it still. I have a harder time, well, then it was just the irritation on me because I would get like dry or whatever it wouldn't feel right, so I never really liked them. And then also knowing that it feels very good, like it feels better for them to not have it on." Rachel, unlike Deborah, still tried to at least occasionally use condoms, even though she preferred sex without them. This was the case for almost all women who disliked condoms. Condom satisfaction, therefore, was one of the dimensions that differentiated women from men as implied users. If men disliked condoms, the couple might struggle to use them. If women disliked them, it might not have mattered.

"I JUST KIND OF ASSUME THAT THAT'S THEIR DUTY"

Investigating the tendency to associate external condoms with men's bodies and men's actions is not simply an interesting exercise. At least part of the reason why women do not bring condoms is their understandings that condoms are a man's method. Indeed, a nationally representative survey conducted by Indiana University and reported on by the New York Times found that 65 percent of women had never even bought a condom.[24] In the present study, just under half of women had not even once brought their own condoms to sexual encounters. Whether the focus is on buying condoms or bringing them, the tendency to treat condoms as the man's method is not inconsequential.

Many women expected men to provide external condoms as a "natural" part of their sexual relationship. Indeed, condom use and their provision by the man "was just assumed" or "automatic," especially in casual relationships. When Bella discussed condom use with her second partner, she said, "I don't know [where he got the condoms]. I just kind of assume that that's their duty. . . . If you're planning on taking a girl home." Olivia (26 years old, Asian) echoed this sentiment, saying "I mean at that time [when learning about sex ed.] I figured if I had a boyfriend, if we need to get one [a condom], it's the guy's responsibility to go to the store and buy one, you know. . . . It's not something I need to worry about. Just make sure they wear them." Thus according to the gendered division of labor that tied external condoms to men's bodies, women like Bella and Olivia did not see it as their responsibility to deal with condoms. Instead, like Nicole (26 years old, white), they were comfortable with the idea that their partners were "kind of in control" of that type of contraception. In fact, one might argue that Olivia's suggestion that her partner go to the store and buy *one condom* is not merely a semantic slip but a concrete reflection of a gender-influenced lack of practical knowledge.

Even when women recognized the tension between feeling sexually empowered and categorizing condoms as a man's responsibility, they might still experience challenges adjusting their behavior. Julie (21 years old, white), described her conversations with one of her partners about condom use, and the thought process that undergirded her approach:

> I think it was like, "Do you have a condom?" And he went and got one and that was kind of like, "Do you want to turn this from what it is [friendship] to sex?" I guess for me it's assumed [that he would have it] but I would not have sex with a guy who didn't want to use a condom. I assume he would have it. And I kind of, I know I should have some of my own, but I expect the guy to provide it. . . . I feel like I should have some [condoms] just to be a modern woman who can take care of herself. But it's easier to let the guy provide it.

Though Julie assumed that the man would provide the condom, therefore, she nonetheless recognized the tension inherent in her position. She considered it important to take care of herself, denoting condom provision as a form of self-protection that was not necessarily linked to sex. But a larger ideology that associates sex with gender and sets cultural expectations for condom provision nonetheless shaped her behavior.

In terms of contraception and STI prevention, assuming that men would provide condoms did not have to lead to complications in sexual encounters—as long as the male partner did indeed bring a condom. As one might imagine, this was not always the case. Some women were adamant about not having sex without a condom, and they refused partners who could not provide one, following the familiar adage "no glove, no love," echoed by Lisa (21 years old, white). Other women in these situations, like Bella, had sex without a condom for various reasons (with varying degrees of discomfort). Bella assumed that condom provision was her partner's "duty." She recounted the times that she had sex with that partner without a condom:

> Yeah, [having sex with him] was fun. It was really carefree and just kind of comfortable. There wasn't any strings attached, and he was also nonreproductive so I didn't have to worry about that. And he was responsible at condoms. We used condoms. Maybe once or twice we didn't but that was just because there weren't any available, and I wasn't really nervous about it because I knew some of his friends and also I couldn't get pregnant. . . . So it was maybe two times that we had sex without me being on birth control, and it was kind of like, "Okay, something happened. Nothing is going to happen. If worse comes to worst, I'm stupid and I get some dumb STD, but I know exactly who it came from."

Bella did not feel concerned about not using condoms with her partner because he had told her he was sterile (they were not relying on her taking birth control for contraception), but she did not discuss the possibility that there was no condom available because neither he nor *she* had brought one. This gendered division of labor around condom provision, and its relationship to tying men's bodies to condoms, has important implications for women's health and reproductive autonomy. In fact, research shows that claiming they do not have a condom available is one of the strategies that some men use to avoid wearing a condom.[25] Thus, although some caution that encouraging women to provide condoms could reinforce their role as sexual gatekeepers and privilege penetrative sex,[26] gendering condoms may unfairly disadvantage women in other ways. This reinforces the importance of considering how gender operates in multifaceted ways in people's everyday lives.

Even when men did provide condoms, women could still be disadvantaged by not providing their own. For example, Josefina (20 years old, Latina) discussed having sex with a casual partner for the first time and the challenges she experienced around condom use after an interruption:

> And so then he was like, "Should I get a condom?" And I'm like, "Yeah." And he's like, "Right now?" And I'm like, "If you want to. We can continue [with foreplay] some more first or whatever." And so he like gets up and gets one and we, you know, we start having sex. . . . And [then his roommate walks in and] he just kind of stands there for a second and he's like, "Oh, sorry." And walks out. I was just like, "What the fuck." And I was like, "I need a moment. Like I'm not really feeling this right now." So like we, you know, sit back and kind of just talk for a little bit and then we start making out again and like, "Okay, can you get a condom?" And so like I'm not paying attention and then I look at him, like a couple, like maybe a minute later and he's like unrolling it or like, you know? . . . And I'm like, "What are you doing?" And he's like, "I need to use this one." And I was like, "You don't have another condom?" . . . And he's like, "No." . . . [So] he used the old condom."

For Josefina, then, assuming that her partner would provide a condom proved problematic only because he had just *one* available. Her incredulity about this demonstrates the pervasiveness of assumptions about gender. In a less gendered system, her partner could have turned the question around on her and asked her if *she* had a condom. Although Josefina was in her partner's room, not providing a condom was not limited to women who engaged in intercourse when they were away from home.

The focus on tying methods to bodies for both women and men also channeled women away from taking an active role in the use of condoms, even when men did provide them. Carolina (26 years old, Latina), reflecting on her experience with condom use in her first relationship, echoed a sentiment similar to that expressed by many other women in the sample—condoms were not something for her to worry about. The conversation excerpted below unfolded when I asked Carolina about her experience with using condoms.

KRYSTALE: And can you tell me, what was the experience of using condoms, was it a hassle for you guys at all, or . . .

CAROLINA: No, it was no hassle for me, I didn't worry about the situation, he did.

KRYSTALE: And can you tell me about how you guys learned about using condoms?

CAROLINA: Who, me, personally?

KRYSTALE: Yeah, you, and then do you know how he learned?

CAROLINA: I don't know how he learned. I have no idea. Me, it was just the fact of like sex ed. or knowing, you know, conversations began with okay, use condoms and make sure you do.

KRYSTALE: And did you feel like you guys knew how to use the condoms correctly?

CAROLINA: I was pretty sure he did. [laughter] I don't, I probably still don't know. I don't worry about that situation. [laughter]

Carolina clearly treated the condom as a method that her partner needed to worry about, even though it would affect both of them were *he* to use it incorrectly. Trisha (22 years old, Black), who was mentioned earlier, similarly said she did not find using condoms difficult to figure out because "I kind of left that up to him. He was more experienced than I was sexually. I knew he knew for the most part what was going on. So I kind of left it up to him because that's all we use. We use the male condoms. So it wasn't like I had to do anything extra. It was more on him to do what he had to do."

Trisha was one of the few women in the study to explicitly mention using "male condoms," strikingly in a context in which she was explaining to the interviewer why she did not spend much time thinking about how to use condoms. Though women assumed dealing with condoms was their partner's responsibility, and were therefore less concerned about whether he used it as intended, correct condom use is particularly important for method effectiveness.[27] For this reason, gendered understandings of external condoms do not have implications only for women's health. These assumptions can limit women's ability to have consensual sexual intercourse on their own terms (that is, intercourse premised on a correctly used condom). They can reinforce existing gendered power differentials within relationships in which men control an important resource and set the terms for sex. And they can erode women's reproductive and bodily autonomy by suggesting a method fundamental to helping them have or not have children on their own terms is not actually *theirs* to "worry about." Thus, though gendered ideologies are taken for granted as natural, it is crucial to interrogate how in contraception they affect knowledge and practice.

Lack of knowledge sometimes created challenges during sexual encounters, even for women who provided their own condoms, as the knowledge that they did have was put to the test. For Montserrat (23 years old, Latina), who preferred to use condoms and the pill simultaneously, a lack of knowledge about the condom contributed to her using "pullout" with a casual partner with whom she had sex a month after meeting him. She said,

> He wanted to pull out instead [of using a condom]. . . . I told him he could stay [inside] because I'm on the pill. He basically like took the condom [off]. He had trouble putting the condom on himself and basically he asked if I could do it and I don't know how to do it. So, he tried and it was difficult and that's when he took it off and we were just not gonna deal with it again. He was just not able to do it. It was just gonna stay without [a condom] and he was like, "I'll pull out." And I told him that it's okay.

Ironically, an experience like Montserrat's demonstrates a fundamental problem with a cultural framework that links the most popular condom to men's bodies—ensuring that women receive less information about their use. Even though Montserrat provided the condom that her partner used, they ended up relying on withdrawal because she did not actually know how to use it.

Increasing the risk of STIs was a critical tradeoff that women like Montserrat made when they and their partners traded condoms for prescription contraception. The next section focuses on how the emphasis on condoms as a "man's method" (versus prescription birth control as a woman's) affected women's experiences in protecting themselves from disease.

"CONDOMS HAVE ALWAYS BEEN A LITTLE SHAKY IN MY HISTORY"

There was widespread concern among public health officials when the CDC released its report on the occurrence of sexually transmitted diseases in the United States in 2015. The report showed that not only had there been increases in the reported number of cases of chlamydia, gonorrhea, and syphilis but the total number of combined cases of the diseases had also reached a historic high.[28] People aged 15–24 accounted for the majority of diagnosed cases of chlamydia and gonorrhea, and the rate of diagnosis for syphilis among women increased more than 25 percent in the one-year period between 2014 and 2015. Consistent with data from previous years, there were racial differences in the rates of STD diagnoses, with Black and American Indian men and women being diagnosed with chlamydia and gonorrhea at higher rates than whites. Though data from the report are no less concerning when contextualized by the analysis that I present in this chapter, they are much less shocking. As I have foreshadowed, and as I show in this section, the way that men and women are differentially channeled into using condoms versus prescription birth control can go a long way toward explaining the challenges around managing STD contraction in the United States.

Perhaps it is not surprising, given that women are channeled toward prescription contraception, that women commonly positioned pregnancy prevention as their most central concern when having sex, whether with casual partners or in monogamous relationships. Discussing their experiences with contraception over the course of their sexual history could trigger on-the-spot reflections on their tendency to be more concerned about pregnancy than about disease. Miranda (28 years old, white), for example, said, "For myself, I have always, always, always thought about [contraception]. I always made sure, to the best of my ability, that I was protected from pregnancy, if not from STDs. Although that's completely [stupid] in a way. You know, condoms have always been a little shaky in my history, but I've always been on something if I was sleeping with somebody." Thus, Miranda always made sure that she was "on something," but because these methods do not prevent STDs, she was less often protected from disease with each of her partners (nine). Ironically, although using condoms more often would have offered her more protection from disease, it could also have offered her more protection from pregnancy. The one pregnancy that she experienced occurred when she used the pill as directed but became pregnant nonetheless, possibly because of method failure and the couple's decision to stop using condoms, on her partner's request, after she began using the pill.

Like Miranda, who had used several methods with her partners, Valentina (22 years old, Latina), was also well versed in contraception, but she wished that she had had more information on STDs previously. She said, "You know, when you talk about birth control, it's just to prevent pregnancies but then like STDs, like until I got into the health care field, [I didn't realize] like there's a lot of STDs, that even can be transmitted even when you wear a condom." As a result of learning about STDs later in life, she wished she had been more careful about using condoms. Her sentiment was echoed by other women. For example, Claire (20 years old, Asian) said, "Thank God I've never gotten an STD or something. That would be terrible. I mean every time I got pregnant [twice], I thought, 'Dude, I should have been smart about it.'" Strikingly, even when reflecting on her wish that she had used condoms to protect herself from disease, she again circled back to wishing she had been "smart[er]" about preventing pregnancy.

Though women overall tended to center pregnancy prevention over disease, Black women tended to be more attuned to the importance of using condoms to avoid contracting sexually transmitted infections. This likely reflects the higher rates of STIs for Black women and their awareness of risk, something that may have felt less tangible for women who had never contracted an STD themselves, or known anyone who had. When Sharon (24 years old, Black) was asked what she would suggest for "making things easier for people to get birth control and condoms and stuff," for example, she said, "I would suggest people use both because it's like condoms don't exactly protect you entirely against pregnancy. There is still a small margin of error and birth control keeps you from getting pregnant, but also condoms keep you from getting diseases and shit. And it's good to be protected from both a pregnancy and diseases, you know." Sharon, in part because of her beliefs about disease, recalled being very assertive with male partners about wearing condoms and felt completely comfortable with buying and carrying her own condoms. In fact, when recalling how she learned about contraception, she said that she learned about it from her mom: "She was very graphic in her sexual education. She blew up pictures of like herpes and was like, 'This is what is going to happen if you don't use a condom.' And I was like, 'Oh, Jesus Christ.'" As a result, when she encountered a partner who was reluctant to buy condoms, she said, "I bought them in the store. He was like, 'I'm too scared.' And I was like, 'You're a fuckin' sissy.'" Sharon's understanding that condoms protected her from both pregnancy and disease, therefore, meant she was more comfortable purchasing and providing them.

For other Black women, even if their mothers never discussed contraception with them (just over 30 percent of women in the sample did not recall ever having a conversation about contraception with their mothers), they were attuned to protecting themselves from disease because of conversations around protection in their communities. Talia (22 years old, Black) discussed the precautions that she took with her partners:

> Yeah, that's with, anybody like, 'cause like, unfortunately, my dudes, we go like, you know how like, majority of the dudes say they don't like using condoms 'cause it take away the feeling and stuff, so like, in order for you to even do that with me, we both gotta go to the doctor. We both going to get checked out and when the tests come back, then we can use, 'cause you know, out here and [my area] period, it's like, STD is like, high risk out here.

Thus, even though Talia did not receive the kind of education from her mother that Sharon did from hers, she was hypervigilant about protecting herself from disease. As she described later in the interview, and as the narratives of other women showed, it was not always easy to ensure her partners wore condoms:

> They like, I'll be like, oh, they start with the kissing and stuff and all that and then the next thing you know, they trying to take off your clothes, then they trying to take off they clothes and then they like, "Okay, I just wanna lay next to you" or they be like, "Turn around" or whatever like they're not gonna do it [try to have sex without a condom], but then they be like, "No, I just wanna stick it in." Just, no, "You can put on this condom," you know what I'm saying. But it ain't no stick it in and pull it out, 'cause that presperm that's coming out holding all them little viruses and STDs you got and you can give it to me. So it's not none of that.

Talia's experience, however, reflects the challenges of assuming that sex with monogamous partners without a condom is safer because they are at lower risk of contracting a disease. Indeed, the one and only time that she contracted an STD, it was gonorrhea from a partner whom she had been in a relationship with for a year and who said he did not know he had it. Like Talia, women of other races also took men's assertions that they did not have a disease at face value.

For other women, even if they cared more about pregnancy than disease when having sex, learning that they had "gotten lucky," or had contracted an STD, often changed their calculations. Women could move from a state of "sexual invincibility" (believing they did not have to worry about contracting a disease) to one of "STD anxiety" (worrying they had symptoms).[29] Ashley (20 years old, white), for example, mentioned how she worried that she might have given her boyfriend an STD because he had an allergic reaction to their latex condom and she had had experience with a "risky" partner in the past:

> I was just paranoid because the whole thing [latex allergy] was going on with my boyfriend. Like when I found out, it was months later that I found out because my friend was ending up like hanging out at these parties that he would go to, but he's [my ex-partner] not allowed in or something. And he would tell me "hey, didn't you do something with him" and I was like, "yeah, a long time ago, why?" and he's like "oh, because he's on the list." And I was like, "what list?" Great.

In other words, Ashley's ex-partner was not allowed into the party because he was on "the list" of people who had an STD. Ashley's experience having sex with this partner, as well as another STD scare she had after having sex without a condom, made her more conscious of the risks that she had taken when she was younger—decisions that she began to question when she had her first serious relationship and worried that an STD could damage it. Similar to Ashley, Barbara (22 years old, white) said, "I mean I wish I had used a condom when I contracted an STD with him." Although several women expressed regret about not using condoms with their partners, they also saw the experiences as an opportunity for growth—whether or not they contracted an STD. As Tiana (21 years old, Black), who contracted a disease from a partner, said, "Some of the experience I do regret of the sex I have, but I feel now it makes me more wise. So when I do find that one that I can get married to, I'm gonna be a little more experienced with sexual things and I'll be more brave to say that I will use protection. I will use condoms or get on the IUD again. I wouldn't use any other form [of prescription birth control], I would just use the IUD." Her experience reflects the ways in which women who had become pregnant as a result of using the pill inconsistently might turn to long-term methods like the IUD if they did not feel empowered to request condoms as a backup.

The experiences of women like Tiana and others highlight the challenges that arise from cultural assumptions that external condoms belong to men. Defining condoms as *male* caused numerous problems for these women's reproductive autonomy. Defining prescription birth control as *female*, however, did not offer women a magic solution. I turn to the challenges that women faced in navigating "their" birth control in the next chapter.

2 Her Birth Control

Scoot down for me . . . open wider . . . that's perfect. I can give you a shot to help with the discomfort . . . I know some women don't like that because they think it's kind of scary to get a shot down there . . . . Okay, you're gonna feel a pinch. . . . That's part of the conversation that I remember having with a doctor when I decided to get a hormonal intrauterine device (IUD) during my second year of graduate school at Stanford. I can still remember my sisters' incredulity when I told them I had gotten not one but *two* shots "down there" to help with the pain of IUD insertion.

The IUD was the fifth method of birth control that I had used with my partner of just over seven years. We started with the shot and condoms, then switched to the pill and condoms after a couple of years, then condoms and spermicide, then back to condoms and the pill, then just condoms, and finally the IUD. I started the shot because that was the method that my older sister used, switched to the pill because the doctor recommended it, switched to condoms and spermicide when I grew tired of the pill, switched back to the pill when I figured I could give a different brand a shot, switched to condoms when I moved for graduate school and would no longer see my partner regularly, and finally switched to the IUD when a staff member at the health center suggested it. She was concerned when I mentioned that my (then) long-distance partner and I used only condoms. What if I got pregnant while trying to complete my PhD program? What would we do living more than four hundred miles apart? Fair point, I mused, and scheduled a referral for an IUD.

This is my experience. Sharing it is consistent with a Black feminist way of knowing, as reflecting on one's position as a researcher is central to a (Black) feminist theory of knowledge.[1] When analyzing the data for this book, I saw both overlap and difference between my and my participants' experiences. A Black feminist way of knowing allowed me to situate my history with prescription birth control use in a broader social context, one in which I recognized that I, too, as a member of the social world, am subject to social forces. I could not, therefore, bracket my own gendered history with prescription birth control as off-limits for analysis.

The analysis of women's narratives revealed that the gendered division of labor in contraception is so pervasive that the term *birth control* itself was often a discursive stand-in for *hormonal birth control*. How does this come to be? Turning to the broader literature provides few answers. While prescription birth control use is nearly ubiquitous, in that most women of reproductive age will use it at some point, the literature is virtually silent on the intimate social processes that shape how women come to use (and discontinue) prescription contraceptives over the life course. Obviously, a desire to prevent pregnancy is central given that the average heterosexual woman will spend approximately thirty years trying to prevent it.[2] *Just Get on the Pill* demonstrates, however, that so is gender. The socially enforced binary in contraception is based in gendered ideologies of appropriate (hetero)sexual behavior for women. Sociologist Katrina Kimport and colleagues refer to this as "normative gendered sexuality,"[3] while other feminist theorists call attention to the role that gender plays in normative heterosexuality in general.[4] *Just Get on the Pill* shows how larger gender ideologies shape women's beliefs that prescription birth control is "their method" in the first place.

Establishing a category of "women's methods" has been a long time in the making. Decades ago, acclaimed scholar Kristin Luker mused that the common prepill methods (condoms and withdrawal) should be thought of as "couple contraceptives" involving different degrees of male participation because both partners have to actively use the methods during sex.[5] She argued that the invention of the pill, an exclusively "female method," dramatically changed the contraception landscape, shifting both responsibility and accountability for pregnancy prevention to women. Indeed, at the time of her writing in 1975, the pill had already outpaced condoms as the method that women most often reported using during their most recent sexual encounter.[6]

Since the publication of *Taking Chances,* the number of methods made for women's bodies has increased dramatically. These include the ring, the shot, the implant, the patch, and a different kind of IUD. No new "male methods" have come to market. Intuition would have it that women often do the heavy lifting in preventing pregnancies and births, using prescription birth control simply because of this historical development. But, as psychologists have shown, our intuitive explanations of the world are usually wrong.[7]

In this chapter, I examine how women come to use prescription birth control with their partners and show that women are supported in using prescription birth control as "their" method by mothers, friends, partners, and medical providers. Though gendering birth control in this way is taken for granted as both natural and beneficial, this chapter shows doing so could create substantial problems for the many women dissatisfied with its use.

"THE NEXT NATURAL STEP IS THAT I START TAKING PILLS"

Mothers and other important women in participants' lives played an important role in shaping their use of prescription birth control, with some figures taking active roles in women's decision making. Vanessa (22 years old, white) recalled how she transitioned from using condoms to using the pill after talking with her mother:

> We used a condom, because my mom, yeah, my mom found it, the [condom] wrapper. [laughter] So I wasn't on birth control at the time, but we did use a condom. And then after that, after the little wrapper thing my mom was like "Oh, you need to go to the doctor. I think we should put you on birth control," and I was like, really, why? And, she was like I found this [the condom wrapper]. And I was like, "We were just trying to see what it looked like on." [laughter] Like I got totally caught. . . . [So] I made the appointment, we made the appointment, so it was like February, so probably like by March I was on birth control because I like got on—see, I would have probably not, but since my mom found out, like she was on top of it [snapping fingers]. . . . She sat in [the doctor's appointment] with me, I had no idea. So it definitely went smoothly with my mom in there. She was kind of like "Okay, we need to put her on birth control," like "What's going on?" "This is going on," and the prescription right there, and we had like a six-month prescription for that [the pill].

Although the experience of getting "caught" mortified Vanessa, her mom assuaged her fears by fully supporting her contraceptive efforts. Her mother's efforts, nonetheless, fall directly in line with gendered expectations of behavior for Vanessa. Vanessa does not recall her mother providing her with additional condoms, or taking her to get condoms of her own, even though it was clear Vanessa had used a condom before. Indeed, while Vanessa's mom later told her that she should keep "using these [condoms] too," she did not aid Vanessa in procuring condoms for herself and Vanessa never brought her own. Ironically, Vanessa later became pregnant while inconsistently taking birth control pills with a casual partner, who preferred not to use condoms. I explore this further in the next chapter.

Though Black women often challenged gendered expectations that they should use prescription birth control over the course of their relationships (as I will discuss in chapter 4), they too recalled being channeled into using prescription methods. Maleyna (28 years old, Black) recounted her mom's efforts to get her to use prescription birth control:

INTERVIEWER: You said that your mom never told you not to have sex. Did she ever tell you about birth control or anything like that?

MALEYNA: Oh, yeah, she actually brought me to Planned Parenthood, I guess when she found out I was having sex. But then I guess the line was too long, so she was just like forget it.

INTERVIEWER: Oh, okay. Do you think she was going to try to get you on the pill?

MALEYNA: I think she was going to get me the IUD—[which is effective] for like five years.

INTERVIEWER: Oh, okay.

Like Vanessa's mom, then, Maleyna's mother actively intervened in trying to get her a prescription form of birth control, but did not take the same initiative with getting her to use a condom. In fact, the differential attention to condom provision is even more striking in Maleyna's case because, while she did not end up getting the IUD because "the line was too long," her mother did not follow up with her to get her condoms. That neither Vanessa's nor Maleyna's family provided condoms for their daughters demonstrates how gender can structure socialization away from condoms and toward hormonal methods. Their and other women's experiences established this was the case across socioeconomic status.

Those women who could not (or did not) talk with their mothers about contraception still recounted having other women in their lives who channeled them toward the pill and other prescription birth control methods. Ashley (20 years old, white) began taking the pill after talking with her friends about having sex. She said, "I think like right when I started dating him is probably when I got the birth control [prescription]. Because like I told my friends and they're like oh, you have to [get on the pill]. So I probably like just started then, but it only lasted two weeks. But I think I started taking it when I was like not really taking it. I was like missing some and just kind of taking it just because my friends told me that I'm supposed to." The gendered expectation that Ashley was "supposed to" start the pill influenced her decision to keep using the method, even if irregularly. The communication of this norm and its reinforcement by her friends are particularly consequential because, even though Ashley conformed to gender expectations by starting the pill, inconsistent use of prescription contraception is directly associated with pregnancy if women are not using a backup method.

In Adrianna's case (29 years old, Black), her sister played a particularly influential role in her decision to begin prescription birth control. Her conversation with the interviewer demonstrated this well:

INTERVIEWER: So, what did she [your sister] tell you? Do you remember that conversation?

ADRIANNA: She said, "You got a little nappy head, little boy running around here." She was like, "You better go see Planned Parenthood." And I'm like, "Who is Planned Parenthood?" And she was like, "The clinic." And she was like, "They ain't gonna tell your mama. They'll call you with a fake name and all this." She was like, "You better go get some birth control." So I went and got the birth control because my other, my best friend that is my friend today, she already knew about Planned Parenthood. . . . So we went there and I got the pill. But my sister, she would say stuff. She was the type of sister that she cut to the chase, she just say it. She'll be like, "You're gonna let that little boy fuck you and make you pregnant? You better go get your ass on some birth control."

As Ashley's and Adrianna's cases show, women got explicit messages about what they "should do" from other women in their lives, either their mothers or someone else. Like participants' mothers, these women helped direct them toward getting the pill but were much less likely to help them strategize about buying or bringing their own condoms.

Even when one woman's brother broke with gender norms to talk with her about the importance of contraception, his message was consistent with larger gendered messages about women's prescription birth control use. Angela (21 years old, Asian) said the following:

> I kind of learned about [contraception] through my brother. I was eighteen. . . . I was online chatting, AIM [AOL Instant Messaging]. He like AIMs me. He's like "have you ever had the talk before, the talk about sex?" I was like, "No. You know our parents. Come on." . . . They don't even try to talk to me about it. So he's like, "Look, you're going to college soon. You might meet someone that you like a lot and you might want to have sex with them." And I was like, "Okay." And he was like, "And when you do, you're eighteen now, you can go get birth control pills. Get them." And he's like, "Also tell them to use a condom. You don't want to get pregnant. Just don't do it." He's like, "I know you're gonna meet someone and you're probably going to like them a lot and you're going to want to [have sex]. So when you do, just make sure you're protected. It's not bad to have sex. Just make sure you don't get pregnant." And I'm like, "Okay." He's almost like a father figure to me because he also took care of me when I was really little, like change[d] my diapers and stuff like that. And so having him say that, it made me feel okay about using it. I didn't look at pills as something that was bad. Like, "Oh, why would you want to take pills?" It's a good way to stay [protected].

While Angela's brother told her to get birth control pills, he did not make the same recommendation about condoms. Instead, he advised her to "tell them to use a condom." Given this messaging, it is perhaps unsurprising that Angela's takeaway from her conversation with him was that using pills is a good idea; it's not "something that was bad." While Angela did get on the pill, she never brought her own condoms.

Because of the effectiveness of prescription birth control, one might wonder whether women are channeled toward using these methods over condoms simply because they are the best means for preventing pregnancy. Though this does not explain why women are not supported in using *both* condoms and prescription birth control (which is actually the most effective strategy),[8] it could be plausible. Women, however, also recounted being encouraged to use less effective "female birth control" methods. Tasha (25 years old, Black), for example, recalled a conversation that she had with her mother about birth control:

> [My mom] was just like, she based it really on what she used. She was like you should look into the diaphragm. And I knew the diaphragm was not the right option for me because I haven't had kids and usually people who use that have kids. Not all the time. And plus birth control pills for me is a lot easier. And, you know, things like that. She probably did mention the birth control pill, condoms and then just going to the doctor to see options and things.

While Tasha decided against using the diaphragm, Deborah (20 years old, white) opted to do so at 16 on the recommendation of her mother until she decided "it's way too messy and gross." In the context of discussing how she learned about contraception from sex ed and her mom, Deborah said the following:

> Yeah, and I guess just talking to my mom about everything. She was the one that suggested that I go down the road of trying a diaphragm because I didn't want any hormones in my body. But yeah, my mom had a big influence. . . . We are so open with each other. About a day after I lost my virginity, I told her about it and the first

question was, "Did he respect you?" Like she is so into female empowerment and she just wanted to make sure that it was something that I really wanted and that I enjoyed it to some degree and so we're very open about all of that and that's why I felt so comfortable telling her about wanting to get some form of birth control. I think I actually got that diaphragm after having lost my virginity and that's when I got my first pap smear and all of that.

As Deborah remarked, her mom played an instrumental role in helping her use a method designed for women's bodies. Deborah wanted to avoid using contraception with hormones because "[she's] predisposed to getting a blood clot and it's not worth it to [her] to risk anything like that." She also is a self-described "naturalist" who doesn't "want hormones that are not [her] own, running through [her] body and controlling [her] period." Thus, although it can be argued that her mom suggested a method that was for women because "she is so into female empowerment," which is indeed likely the case, there is no reason why her mom had to suggest the diaphragm—a method less effective than the condom—as a method that her daughter could use to avoid putting hormones in her body. Indeed, there is no reason why suggesting the condom to her daughter needed to be any less empowering than suggesting the diaphragm, especially since condoms protect against both STIs and pregnancy. Like Tasha, Deborah ended up using other forms of hormonal birth control (the patch), but, perhaps related to the kinds of messages that she received, she never provided her own condoms and was one of the minority of women to use withdrawal as her main form of birth control.

Lastly, women also discussed sharing hormonal methods and information on hormonal methods much more often than they discussed sharing condoms, which was largely understood as something that men did. Several women mentioned providing emergency contraception and prescription birth control pills to their friends, but women less often bought condoms for each other. Amanda (21 years old, white) even waited for "like two hours" at a clinic, where she had to "do all this crap and it was just like so much work," to get emergency contraception for a friend. Women discussed giving each other prescription birth control as if it were unproblematic in every case in which they discussed sharing prescription methods with others. In one of the few instances in which women mentioned sharing condoms, however, Carolyn (21 years old, white) said she "had some randomly that [her] friends had given [her] as a joke." Women, in other words, would go to clinics to get emergency contraception for their friends, stock up on it for each other "just in case," and even trade pills in the event that one of them had a prescription that had run out, but they never jokingly gave each other hormonal methods.

Given the broader gendered messages about contraception, it is unsurprising that when the prospect of having sex arose women often began making plans to get prescription contraception (and not condoms) as part of their protection strategy. Valentina (22 years old, Latina), for example, recounted that there was never a time when she wished she had used contraception, saying "I just always faced reality and was like if I'm having sex there can be a possibility that I'm getting pregnant. So I just went ahead and made sure that if I am having sex, I need to protect myself and I always used [prescription] birth control." As previously mentioned, women also took initiative in using other less effective "female" birth control methods, adhering to gender norms even as the methods offered less protection from pregnancy.

Women often thought of "getting on birth control" as the next logical step in the sexual script, but their behaviors also demonstrated that gender expectations shaped their decisions and not just a particularly strong motivation to avoid pregnancy. Take the experience of Gina (23 years old, white):

> INTERVIEWER: Did you guys ever have conversations about birth control?
>
> GINA: Yeah, I mean it was like sort of a process we were doing together. So it was like, "I'm starting [the pill] now. It'll be effective in a month. We should use condoms until then. Blah, blah, blah."
>
> INTERVIEWER: So you brought it up to him?
>
> GINA: I mean I think we were talking about it together. We both wanted to have sex. The next natural step is that I start taking pills.
>
> INTERVIEWER: Okay. And at what point of the relationship did this talk happen?
>
> GINA: Maybe four months.
>
> INTERVIEWER: Okay. So before the sex?
>
> GINA: Of course. Yeah. That would be funny if it would be after?

For Gina, the prospect of even having sex required that she begin using hormonal birth control. The idea that she would discuss the pill only after having sex seemed laughable to her. Typical explanations of gendered patterns of birth control use center the effectiveness of the pill in motivating her behavior. In general, the pill is "the next natural step" because women are highly motivated to prevent pregnancy and the pill is among the most effective methods. This approach, as demonstrated for women's use of "less effective female methods," overlooks the important role that understandings of bodies can play in motivating women to use (or not use) particular methods with their partners. As a consequence, this perspective cannot explain why Gina ended up using emergency contraception because she and her partner had sex without a condom *before* her birth control became effective. Elaborating the ways that women used highly effective methods because they were designed for their bodies, however, can shed light on behavior that appears inconsistent when concerns over method effectiveness are centered as the only metric that women use in their contraceptive decision making.

At other times, women's difficulty in explaining why they chose *not* to use prescription birth control helped demonstrate the pervasiveness of gendered beliefs that hold women should use particular methods. Trisha (22 years old, Black) had difficulty explaining her reasoning for consistently refusing to use birth control to her interviewer:

> Earlier last year, I went to the doctor for the whole checkup thing, yearly thing. And they suggested that because they went on my sexual history and they suggested that I try birth control again and I was thinking about it. I thought about it. I thought about it like do I need it or do I really want to be on birth control, any type, and I eventually just decided against it. Why? I don't know why, actually. I don't know why. I don't know, actually. I don't know why. I just decided against it. I just decided not to use birth control. I felt like I was doing well with the condoms so I guess that's what it was.

It is fascinating that Trisha needed several sentences to explain to the interviewer that she refused to begin prescription birth control because she did not *need* it. Her discomfort may be a consequence of what researchers Emily Mann and Patrick Grzanka call "agency without choice," whereby women are taught that using prescription birth control (long-acting methods in their study) is the only logical choice if they want to prevent pregnancy.[9] The notion that women felt as though they needed to justify not using prescription birth control with their monogamous partners is striking, in that they never justified stopping condom use after beginning prescription birth control with these partners. Indeed, as I show in the next chapter, stopping was seamless for many women, who saw it as unproblematic. Before turning to that discussion in chapter 3, however, I first demonstrate how consistent prescription birth control use itself could be trying for women because of the centrality of dissatisfaction.

"ALL BIRTH CONTROL MAKES YOU CRAZY" AND OTHER CHALLENGES

Prescription birth control was not inconsequential for women to use. It could be costly. It could be inconvenient. It could even be dissatisfying. Indeed, my own research using a nationally representative survey showed that nearly 40 percent of women who had ever used hormonal birth control had stopped it at some point because of dissatisfaction.[10] Strikingly, other researchers found that 91 percent of women believed that no available birth control method (prescription or other) had all of the characteristics that they considered extremely important.[11] Black, Latina, and Asian Pacific Islander women are also more likely than white women to emphasize the extreme importance of being able to stop their method immediately when evaluating contraceptive methods.[12] Few prescription birth control methods offer this option. While prescription contraception is commonly understood as an ideal solution when men dislike condoms, cisgender women have their own frustrations with the birth control method assigned to their sex. In this section, I shed light on women's dissatisfaction with prescription contraception, centering their narratives about side effects as the central cause of discontent.

There is mixed evidence of a connection between prescription birth control and weight gain, with studies showing a link for some methods but not others.[13] Regardless of whether prescription contraception actually caused weight gain, the perception that it did sometimes led women to stop, switch, or steer clear of prescription birth control methods altogether. Sharon (24 years old, Black) talked about the side effects that she had when she used the pill. She said, "I went on high hormone pills, which made me really fucking fat and I hated it. And then I went on the patch." Later in the interview, she elaborated on some of the other side effects that she experienced:

SHARON: Yeah. I got really fat when I used the pill. When I used Depo ["the shot"], a lot of the weight shed off, like a lot. I didn't have, when I was on Depo, I didn't have the emotional shit but I did have it when I was on the pill. For the most part, yeah. The only side effects I had were from the pills that they had in the little, that circular coral thing.

INTERVIEWER: So how did you know it was caused by birth control?

SHARON: I wasn't like that before. I wasn't angry or irritable. I was like laid back and relaxed all the time. I didn't care about like a lot of things and then stupid shit would get me pissed off [on the pill], you know.

Like Sharon, many women relied on their embodied knowledge (the knowledge gained through trusting their bodily experience) to determine that their birth control caused side effects. They often used changes in their behavior or experience before and after they started using a method as evidence that their birth control was the culprit.

Women also tried to combat the changes and only concluded that prescription birth control caused them when they found no relief. In this lengthier exchange with an interviewer, Brianne (21 years old, white) discussed her experience with weight gain while using the contraceptive implant and the challenges that she had with negotiating removal:

BRIANNE: Yeah. So I had it. I actually had that in me for five months and I got acne. My face just completely broke out. It was disgusting. I got acne, I gained weight. So within a five month period, I gained twenty pounds.

INTERVIEWER: Wow.

BRIANNE: And it was way difficult to get off. So I got that removed. I got completely off of it. I lost like two pounds and that was it. And then I did the patch. I didn't gain weight. I think I got hungry on the patch. But I can control my [hunger] for the most part, so I was okay. And it [would] just keep coming off.

INTERVIEWER: So it didn't work.

BRIANNE: Yeah. But Depo, no side effects from Depo.

INTERVIEWER: Okay. And can you tell me like how you knew it was the birth control giving you side effects and how you decided whether or not you wanted to stop taking it?

BRIANNE: Well, I started realizing that, at first I was gaining weight and I was like, "Okay, this is not working out right now."

So I started working out. I was working out really hard and yet, I wouldn't lose any weight and I was still gaining and it didn't make any sense. At first I thought it was just muscle because that's what always happens to me. But no, I just kept gaining. I was like, "This is not right." I had acne and I just ke[pt] thinking about everything and I was like looking back at the day I started and I was like, "That's when everything began." And I was really emotional. So I decided to take it out and then I had it removed and two weeks later my face cleared up.

INTERVIEWER: Wow.

BRIANNE: Yeah. And then the weight, I didn't lose it but I stopped gaining. I was not gaining weight from then on.

INTERVIEWER: And did you talk to your doctor at all about getting off of it or did you just decide that you just wanted out and that was it?

BRIANNE: Oh, yeah. They're like, "You know, no one ever gains weight on this and no one gets acne. You know, a small percentage. And everyone likes this." And I was like, "I don't care. Take it out now." Like, everyone's body is clearly different. So they did.

There is debate about whether clinicians should tell women about harder-to-measure side effects (called nonspecific side effects) that have not been definitively proved by clinical trials for fear women may inaccurately attribute bodily changes to prescription birth control.[14] Women's discussions, however, suggested that their doctors' thoughts were only one factor that they used to determine whether their birth control caused side effects. In Brianne's case, her doctor's beliefs had no impact on her decision to discontinue use once exercise failed to result in weight loss.

Fear that a method *could* lead to weight gain was also a strong enough motivation to prevent some women from considering prescription birth control. Paulina (21 years old, Latina) talked with me about the many challenges that prevented her from using the pill. After I asked her to "tell me a little bit more [about how] like you refused getting on [prescription] birth control," she responded,

> I don't know. My sister is on birth control. She has always been on it. I mean with it, she still gets pregnant. She is like very fertile. I don't know. I just refused to get on it because like before they came out with the shots or everything else that's not a pill, it's like I have so much going on in my life that I would forget to have to take it at the same time, like every day. And then it wouldn't be effective, so it would be a waste, a waste of money, a waste of whatever. Also, like I heard they [pills] make you gain weight unnecessarily. And like all these things that I feel that I can do without, and just using a condom. And also like using birth control like, if a guy knows you're honest, like "Oh well, then I cannot use a condom." But because I had so many like scares of like STIs, like I just use a condom all the time now. If I'm going to use a condom anyway, then I don't need to be on birth control.

Paulina's explanation demonstrates the importance of considering the larger social context in which women must navigate using prescription birth control. Her association of the pill with weight gain and her discomfort with using it every day made it a less viable option for her. Instead, she preferred to use condoms.

As I have discussed in my previous work,[15] concerns about weight gain often go hand in hand with concerns about emotional volatility as women struggle to navigate gendered expectations of behavior when experiencing side effects. Women like Vanessa (22 years old, white), who experienced intense mood swings on birth control, had challenges not only figuring out that it was their birth control that caused the side effects but also determining what they should do about it. While Vanessa described herself as generally "pretty like laid back," she felt as though the pill made her "moody" and "freak out." Vanessa switched birth control methods after noticing that she felt "nuts" the first time she used the pill. She struggled to find a brand that completely resolved the problem, however. Even though the pill that she was using at the time of the interview was "by far like not bad," she still characterized the week before her period in the following way: "You're just such an ass, like you are just so not nice to people . . . like when I wasn't on birth control like I don't think I was this much of a, you know, a brat like that week before. Because I know sometimes I just want, like I'm just like so just stay away, don't come near me, please, please don't touch me." Vanessa was much more satisfied with the pill at the time of the interview. Because of her own experience, she nonetheless concluded "all birth control makes you kind of crazy."

Strikingly, women's perceptions of mood changes could make them feel like side effects changed who they were as people. Lindsey (20 years old, white) tried at least two different pills because she was "just sort of nauseous" and "just like a mess, moody, etcetera etcetera" for the first month of use. She was considering the IUD at the time of the interview, as she had learned more about her prescription birth control options. While Lindsey did not immediately find a pill that she could tolerate, she still felt fairly happy with her experience. When the interviewer remarked on Lindsey's general satisfaction with birth control and asked if there were anything that she might want to change, Lindsey responded,

LINDSEY: Yeah. I mean, I was on the lightweight crew team and you never really know if [that is] the reason I couldn't lose the weight. I couldn't lose the weight so I had to switch to open weight. So I never know if the reason I couldn't lose the weight was because I was on birth control or because I wasn't disciplined enough, whatever, whatever, or just my body didn't want to do it. So that's like one thing I'm sort of like, like I said, I'm really curious to see what I would be like without the pill. Would I personally be different? You know, hormone changes, the way you act and feel and react to things or would I lose weight? Would it be easier to lose weight, gain weight, whatever. Would my boobs shrink? You know what I mean?

INTERVIEWER: Yeah, yeah. When you first went on the pill did you gain weight?

LINDSEY: See, that's the thing. I'm not sure because I was dieting all the time because I was five pounds over and then my weight kind of went up. So maybe, but I was also lifting weights. So I'm not really sure. My boobs definitely grew but it could have just been an age thing. They grew like an inch. I'm not sure.

INTERVIEWER: Okay. Cool.

LINDSEY: I think so because my sister's boobs are really big and mine were never this big, so it probably has to do with the pill a little bit.

As the exchange demonstrates, even though Lindsey did not find the weight gain and mood changes that she experienced so intolerable that she wouldn't try other oral contraceptives, reflecting on the side effects made her wonder if the pill made her behave like a different person. It also made her question whether she simply lacked the "grit" that she needed to successfully lose weight. Thus, women's perceptions of weight gain and emotional volatility mattered not only because of gendered notions of attractiveness or emotional instability but also because such experiences shaped how they evaluated themselves as people and determined whether or not they achieved important nonfertility-related goals in their lives.

Even as women tried to achieve their fertility goals while having sex, they might have had to manage side effects that affected their libido and relationships. When Bella (21 years old, white) stopped using her birth control method, it created additional stress because she and her boyfriend did not always use condoms after she stopped. She said, "I had a couple of two- or three-day scares. I did go off the NuvaRing for a month while we were dating because it started to, what's that word, started to deter my sex drive. Like I didn't want sex and wanted to see if that was the cause basically. It was making my emotions a little bit weird. And I took Plan B [emergency contraception] and everything was fine besides a week of being nervous. Besides that, I didn't have any pregnancy scares." Bella eventually resumed use and also tried the pill to see if oral contraception might work better for her.

Teresa (26 years old, Latina), on the other hand, did not stop using birth control when her libido changed, but she said she experienced pressure from her boyfriend to do so "because I didn't have a [sex] drive either because of hormones. He usually gets upset because he would think that I would be doing it on purpose because I didn't want to do it [have sex] or it is just like, I couldn't control the way that my body reacted and so there was conflict in that sense." Interestingly, Teresa referred explicitly to what sociologist Arlie

Hochschild called "emotion work" in her canonical 1983 book on the commercialization of emotion.[16] While workers like flight attendants and others are paid to manage emotional displays in the public sphere, women like Teresa had to do emotion work to manage side effects that affected their moods or libido. Indeed, Teresa and her boyfriend had problems not because she did not have a sex drive but because she could not do the emotion work necessary to "control the way that [her body] reacted"—that is, she could not make herself *feel* interested in sex. Though women's emotion management in pregnancy prevention is often overlooked, the refusal of women in this study to do emotion work or have sex when they lacked "a drive" highlighted how such non-normative behaviors had consequences for their reproductive autonomy. When the interviewer asked Teresa if her boyfriend wanted her to stop taking the pill, for example, Teresa said the following:

> Yeah, because it clearly made a difference with the whole, yeah, it made a difference within our sex lives because I just no longer wanted to be . . . I might even know I didn't want to do it. It is just like; physically my body didn't really [want it]. . . . I would just tell him, "I'm sorry, I think it's the birth control." He thought I was lying but I know it's the fact that that is one of the side effects. He just really didn't take it well.

Thus, women like Teresa sometimes experienced challenges when it came to side effects, but not necessarily because of their own discomfort with side effects or because of the emotion work required. Instead, they intended to stay on birth control to protect themselves from pregnancy, but this also potentially meant having to navigate conflict with their partners.

Navigating sexuality with sexual partners could prove particularly challenging if women experienced side effects that affected menstruation. If the changes were minor, many women persisted. In fact, some women even enjoyed what they considered positive effects like lighter (or no) periods. Manuela (22 years old, Latina), for example, thought having her period for a single day as a result of her being on the pill was a "blessing." For other women, however, the changes were negative and posed too much of a nuisance for them to continue. Lauren (23 years old, white) discussed why she might consider resuming use of "the shot":

Oh, I did the Depo, the shot. I did that and so, I did the shot. I remember that was the first birth control method I tried. It was good and actually I think I might go back to it because, the reason why, like I didn't want to go back was because I had spotting. So I was always having to wear a tampon because I hate wearing pads. But now I'm old enough to know, like, it's okay to wear a pad and I don't wear thongs anymore. I just wear the Hanky Pankies [briefs]. I don't wear the G-strings and thongs like I did in high school.

As she explained, Lauren actually liked using the shot (especially because she preferred intercourse without condoms), but spotting every day made continuing its use undesirable. Her challenges trying to negotiate prescription birth control use while wearing "G-strings and thongs" also demonstrated the challenges she faced trying to enjoy her sexuality in relationships while using the method that was supposed to give her more sexual freedom.

As Teresa's and Lauren's experiences highlight, women used many strategies to manage prescription birth control use when they had side effects. They might talk with doctors about switching methods, talk with friends or boyfriends to try and help them understand their experiences, or simply adopt habits that made it easier to deal with the side effects. Maite (23 years old, Latina), for example, strategized about *when* she took her birth control. When Maite realized that the pill made her feel nauseated, she decided to keep using it until her body adjusted to the hormones. To manage the nausea in the meantime, she said, "So I got in the habit of taking my birth control pill at night so that I could just go to sleep and like, sleep through any discomfort." Maite's strategy of "waiting it out" was a common tactic, and one recommended by clinicians, since side effects often resolve by themselves over time. How long side effects take to resolve can differ for each person, however. It took over a month for Maite to stop feeling nauseated. It took Maya (23 years old, Black) a bit longer. She talked about her experience using the IUD with the interviewer:

INTERVIEWER: Oh, you had that [the IUD].

MAYA: Yeah, 'cause I had a Shrek dream. I don't know if you seen that movie where Shrek is about to have a baby and all the bab[ies] start coming through the window. I had the same dream but it was like my son and daughters and everyone coming through the window. So that kind of freaked me out. So I went to go get it.

INTERVIEWER: When did you get it then? It was after you broke up with your son's father or during?

MAYA: No, it was after. Like after we broke up, after the abortion, that's when I went to go get it. Like, I had the dream. I think it was after I met [my next partner], afterwards.

INTERVIEWER: Okay. So when you were with [your partner] is when you had it?

MAYA: Um-hm.

INTERVIEWER: Okay. So you weren't too worried about it [pregnancy] 'cause you had the IUD.

MAYA: Um-hm.

INTERVIEWER: And how was the IUD? Like how was it for you?

MAYA: The first like three months, I didn't like it. It gave me really bad cramps and my period was even more severe. I didn't like it. Afterwards, I forgot about it and everything else. It's working now.

INTERVIEWER: You still have it now?

MAYA: Um-hm. I think they said you can leave it in five to ten years. But I don't think it'll be in that long. It's kind of disgusting to have something like that in you.

INTERVIEWER: For that long.

MAYA: Yes. So, I don't know. But it's been a year, I think. A year and a half, almost two years. So it's been working out.

For Maya, tolerating severe cramps and a more severe period may have felt particularly worth it for her because she could use the method for such a long period of time, though she noted that she did not necessarily intend to use it for as long as the manufacturer recommends. While some women stopped prescription birth control use altogether, most eventually tried another form. Indeed, resilience was one of the consistent themes in the study. In the words of Rachel (26 years old, white), even when women felt scared, dissatisfied, or apprehensive, many still ended up "working up the guts" to try again. As other researchers have contended, women performed an important form of physical and emotional labor in helping their partners prevent pregnancy,[17] despite their dissatisfaction, and providers could contribute to channeling them toward particular methods.[18] *Just Get on the Pill* demonstrates how family and friends, too, contributed to socializing women into this work. The next chapter turns to how the gendered division of labor could create inequity in women's quest to prevent pregnancy.

3   *Don't Be a Bitch*

Nearly a century ago, an esteemed doctor noted that "the sheath [external condom] maintains its conspicuous place as the best known and simplest measure [to prevent pregnancy]."[1] Nonetheless, he continued, "It is very commonly refused by the feebly virile and the selfish."[2] Today, the language has changed, but the underlying message remains largely the same: though technically effective, the condom is less reliable for contraception. Dominant logic holds that monogamous couples should use prescription birth control (for women) instead. Researchers, for example, explicitly addressed one of the central challenges of condom use in a 2017 article in one of the premier journals for sexual and reproductive health. They proposed "female-controlled" methods as the solution. Following are the abstract's opening sentences: "Heterosexually active men who wish to prevent conception, but are not willing to use condoms consistently, need to discuss birth control with female partners. Improving the understanding of correlates of men's intention to have such discussions is one step toward supporting this health-facilitating behavior."[3] Having men who do not want to wear condoms talk to their female partners about using prescription contraceptives might indeed reduce the chances of couples' conceiving because of infrequent condom use, but what are the consequences of legitimizing this logic for women's sexual health and reproductive autonomy?

In this chapter, I move from examining gendered understandings of birth control to more explicitly examining the consequences of these ideologies for gendered health inequity and bodily autonomy. Though improving the use of highly effective methods of birth control has been upheld as the solution to a variety of social ills, this social imperative has a variety of unintended consequences. Drawing on women's narratives of preventing pregnancy and birth, I show how gendering contraception supports a compulsory birth control system for women—in interactions with their partners, their families, and their doctors. This analysis sheds light on how assumptions about gender that shape contraceptive practices encroach on women's ability to freely choose their birth control methods. It can also make it difficult for them to prevent pregnancy when they are channeled into choosing prescription birth control over "male" methods like condoms, which may better suit them. This runs contrary to assertions that gender inequality is an unfortunate, but beneficial, feature of prescription contraceptive use.

PREVENTING PREGNANCY, PRODUCING INEQUITY

Social science research on gender and contraception typically operates under the umbrella of *social reproduction*, a term used by feminist researchers to refer to the activities, behaviors, and responsibilities that contribute to reproducing and maintaining life on a daily basis.[4] Social reproduction research focuses on work and the (gender-based) division of labor. Previous chapters followed closely in this tradition by illuminating how understandings of gender mattered for the division of birth control into methods for men and methods for women. In this chapter, I move from a narrower focus on gender norms to a broader focus on how social structures create inequity.

Structures are composed of cultural frameworks that help guide behavior, as well as resources intended to serve as tools for people to generate power on the basis of the cultural frameworks prevalent in a society.[5] The key is that cultural frameworks themselves help determine which objects or skills count for gaining power. Through this lens, birth control methods qualify as a resource only in a context with frameworks that celebrate preventing and delaying pregnancy (i.e., "family planning"). Whether prescription birth control serves to enhance or maintain women's power, however, depends on the other cultural frameworks in operation. When contexts also have frameworks that position women as the bearers of responsibility for preventing births, as I show in this chapter, prescription birth control can become an object that *erodes* women's power over their bodies and self-determination, even as it helps them avoid pregnancy.[6] In the sections that follow, I show how gendered ideologies can make prescription birth control use compulsory for women, decreasing women's ability to use it as the resource that people largely assume that it is.

Gendered Compulsory Contraception

Gender need not be problematic so long as it does not encroach on people's ability to do what they wish; in practice, however, that is exactly what gendered structures do across a variety of contexts.[7] Although several women discussed prescription birth control as a way of "protecting themselves," as discussed in the previous chapter, birth control use could take on a compulsory edge when male partners suggested to avoid using condoms. Laura (26 years old, Latina), for example, discussed how she transitioned from using condoms to using the birth control pill with her partner:

> INTERVIEWER: The first time you had sex with him, did you use a condom?
>
> LAURA: Yes. Yes.
>
> INTERVIEWER: Were you the one who initiated or was it him? How did that conversation go?
>
> LAURA: Um, I think if I hadn't brought it up, I don't think he would have used a condom.
>
> INTERVIEWER: Okay. Were you using any other protection, like the birth control pill or the shot?
>
> LAURA: It was my first time having sex, so I just, the condom was the first thing that I knew to protect myself and then afterwards, he was the one who mentioned, "Oh, yeah, get on the pill."
>
> INTERVIEWER: Okay. Do you remember any times when you used contraception and also you didn't use contraception?
>
> LAURA: No, we always used something.
>
> INTERVIEWER: Okay. Did you ever have any conversations or conflicts over using it?
>
> LAURA: He didn't like using condoms, so that's why I had to get on the pill and the other stuff, the patch and I also took the shot.

Laura's decision to begin using the pill is in line with public health recommendations that women hoping to avoid pregnancy use prescription birth control.[8] Laura's case, however, highlights the challenges inherent in a perspective that centers only the effectiveness of prescription birth control without also providing contextual information on how gender shapes contraceptive negotiation. Though Laura and her partner began using the pill for contraception, the decision stemmed from a place of unequal power—that is, her partner assumed that she should use prescription birth control, but the decision, in fact, may not have felt particularly empowering for her. Indeed, Laura recounts getting on the pill as something she "had to" do, not something that she particularly wanted to do.

Like Laura, other women casually mentioned resorting to prescription birth control because of their partner's resistance to condoms. Rachel (26 years old, white), for example, did not view using hormonal birth control as particularly problematic, even though she did so in response to her boyfriend's refusal to wear condoms after their first child was born. She said, "Yeah, after I had my son, I was put on the pills. I couldn't tell you which ones they were, though, okay, but I went on the pill. Then I stopped but we weren't having sex, really, anymore anyway. And then I got an IUD and so that way I don't even have to worry about anything." It felt logical for Rachel to get an IUD because not using anything—which is what she and her partner did before they transitioned to the IUD— was stressful and she often forgot to take the pill. Nonetheless, her feeling that she had to use an IUD to avoid pregnancy was not without negative consequences for Rachel, even though it virtually eliminated her chances of getting pregnant. In fact, when discussing her satisfaction with contraception later in the interview, Rachel said, "I wish there was a male birth control, I really do. Instead of it always being our kind of responsibility, let it be theirs. Seeing as they're the ones who kind of complain about birth, you know, certain kinds of birth control more than us, I think it should be their responsibility, as well." Contrary to some who assert that "birth control for men" is unviable because women would not trust them to use it,[9] women like Rachel expressed a desire for just this kind of support in preventing pregnancy. While Rachel may be protected from pregnancy in the short-term, it is not unreasonable to believe that frustration over contraception "always being her responsibility" could at some point lead her to reject prescription birth control.

Women's experiences of being channeled into using "female methods" because their partners did not want to wear condoms was not limited to highly effective birth control. Some women recounted using emergency contraception, which may not always prevent pregnancy. Audrey (20 years old, white) and her boyfriend, for example, often had sex without condoms when she was not taking hormonal birth control because he preferred not to wear them, which she understood because "having a condom can be difficult for a guy sometime." She first learned about emergency contraception from him. When discussing why she had not felt concerned about getting pregnant with him, she said, "Then, no [I was not concerned]. I think because the problem is [previously] I was in a relationship where you just use condoms. There was never an issue and then of course I was like, 'Oh, they have this Plan B thing. It should work.' He told me [that]. But it should. It usually does, apparently." As Audrey alluded to here, emergency contraception did *not* work for her, and she experienced a pregnancy with this partner: "But he [had] been understanding. Like, he was understanding about the pregnancy." Poignantly, even when Audrey's pregnancy resulted from 1) her partner's refusing to wear condoms, and 2) her use of a method that *he* told her would work, she still accepted responsibility for it. As evidence, in reflecting on her experience getting pregnant, Audrey wondered if she "could have taken the [daily] pill" to avoid it. She eventually tried using the pill after the pregnancy, when she and her partner continued having sex without a condom. As Audrey's example shows, even when women had successfully used condoms in long-term relationships and would have preferred to use them with their current partners, they might still have been compelled to use so-called women's methods for avoiding pregnancy, rather than those understood as men's methods. Though doing so might have helped them to prevent pregnancy, it could also have contributed to subordinating their needs and autonomy in the relationship. As Audrey said at the end of the interview, when discussing times when she had not used any form of contraception with her partner, "There have been times when he and I have had the same thing happen [had to use emergency contraception] and it's almost like the same situation. I was like, 'Oh, technically we should have learned from this.' . . . I just think men. Maybe that's what a lot of people might say, 'Oh, I wasn't thinking.' It [sex] almost becomes less about thinking about yourself and mostly about being with him, which isn't necessarily a healthy thing." In this case, Audrey's comments reflect the idea that gender-normative behavior for women in heterosexual relationships often included centering men's needs, and "being with him" meant having sex on his terms—without a condom. This analysis builds on the work of other scholars focusing on norms and normatively gendered sexuality by demonstrating how women's gender-normative behavior in one dimension (centering partners) could lead to gender *non-normative* behavior in another (not contracepting).[10]

For other women, the challenge was not deciding whether or not to begin using prescription birth control but figuring out how to avoid carrying the burden for contraception singlehandedly once they did so. Isabella (21 years old, Asian) described how she had to negotiate condom use with her boyfriend once she began taking the pill:

> Once he was like, "I think we should not use the condom." Because it was hurting and stuff like that. And I was like, "Yeah. Well, I'm on the pill so it should be fine." But when we started, we were like kissing and stuff like that and then I wasn't feeling that comfortable. I just didn't want to . . . [but] he just asked, "Well, aren't you on the pill? That should be enough." And I was like, "Yeah. But please. I don't exactly know how this thing works. I've never taken the pill before or anything. So can you just please?" And he was [like], "Okay."

Isabella's boyfriend's knowledge of her pill use nearly led the couple to have sex without a condom (during a period when she had only recently started taking the pill daily) because he assumed if she was "on the pill," then he did not have to wear a condom. Isabella's ability to push back against her partner's attempts to make them rely solely on "her birth control" for pregnancy prevention saved her from worrying about pregnancy later, but other women were not so lucky. Thus, while using hormonal birth control could help couples avoid pregnancy when one partner resisted condom use, it could also potentially make it more difficult by giving resistant partners "a reason" not to wear condoms.

Perhaps as a consequence of the shifting of responsibility for contraceptive use after the commencement of prescription birth control, women's decisions to start and then stop use could also create challenges for their reproductive autonomy as partners refused to return to using condoms. Holly (20 years old, white) recalled having fights with her boyfriend, saying "He was just like, 'Well, you should just go back on birth control and then we don't need to worry about using a condom all the time.' And I was like, 'Well, you should just use a condom all the time and we don't have to worry about anything.' And he got mad at me and was like, 'You're a bitch.'" The idea that Holly should use the pill is in line with gendered expectations that women use a method designed for their bodies. The notion that she is a *bitch* because she would not, however, demonstrates how gender as a social phenomenon structuring inequality could generate pressure on women to use prescription birth control, not because it is highly effective, but because it allows men to avoid using a method assigned to their sex. In fact, at least one woman remarked that she refused to tell casual partners that she was taking the birth control pill to avoid conversations about whether or not they needed to wear a condom.

Though it was less common, a number of women used emergency contraception after having unprotected intercourse because their partners removed the condom without their knowledge. In these cases, women's experiences reflect the epitome of gendered compulsory contraception: they literally had no other choice but to take emergency contraception if they wished to circumvent pregnancy. Their stories also demonstrate how coercion and pain could underlie even those sexual experiences that women labeled consensual.[11] In fact, a nontrivial minority of women in the study discussed men who either did not use or removed condoms without their consent. Ann (27 years old, Asian) described the circumstances that led her to use Plan B:

KRYSTALE: Can you tell me about those times when you guys didn't use condoms? Can you tell me how that happened? Like how did you guys end up not using a condom?

ANN: He can't find any condoms and then, hm, and then we have sex without [a] condom.

KRYSTALE: Okay.

ANN: The first time he did that, I didn't know he wasn't using condoms.

KRYSTALE: I see. How did you feel about that?

ANN: I was mad.

KRYSTALE: So he just didn't tell you? So he just kind of, you thought he was getting a condom?

ANN: I mean he took it off at some point and I didn't notice. So I was [like], "Are you using it? Are you?" He didn't use anything and he already finished [ejaculated].

As a result of having sex without a condom, Ann went to a clinic and got a prescription for emergency contraception. She considered breaking up with him, but she said, "He regretted it [taking the condom off] and used condoms most of the time. So it was okay."

In addition to revealing the inequity inherent in compelling women to use hormonal birth control, Ann's boyfriend's decision to remove the condom without her consent is also problematic along another dimension: Ann (and other women) actually preferred not to use hormonal birth control. Nonetheless, like Audrey, who decided to try the pill after repeatedly having unprotected sex with a boyfriend who refused to wear a condom, Ann said that if she could not use a condom, then her "second choice is the pill." Thankfully, because of the pill, women like Ann had recourse to other contraception when they encountered partners who refused to wear condoms. This fact, however, renders pill use no less compulsory and nonconsensual condom removal no less serious as a form of gendered violence.[12]

While women's discussions of gendered compulsory contraception often centered on negotiations of contraceptive use with partners, medical providers could also play an important role in channeling them toward "female" and away from "male" birth control methods. These strategies have important implications for method adoption and patterns of use. In the excerpt below, note how Gina's doctor assumed she would have unprotected sex were she to discontinue using the pill and then met someone she wanted to have sex with. After breaking up with her boyfriend, Gina (23 years old, white) considered stopping use of the pill but decided against it. When explaining why she continued its use, she said, "I went to my gynecologist. I will not forget this. I told him, 'You know, I just broke up with my boyfriend. Maybe I should stop the pills. I know there are hormones.' And he's like, 'You know, Gina, what if you like wake up tomorrow and prince charming on the white horse will come and pick you up? What will you do if you won't be on birth control pills? You must get birth control pills. Stay on them.' So I was like, 'Okay.'" As Gina alluded, it was not unusual for women to stop using prescription birth control when they ended relationships with boyfriends or long-term casual partners. What her doctor's advice suggested, however, is that she must continue using the pill if she wanted to uphold her end of the bargain if "prince charming" came along—presuming that he would want to immediately have sex without a condom and that her job would be to accept (and be prepared for) that eventuality. In her words, she interpreted the doctor as saying that "the risk of having unprotected sex is a lot bigger than, you know, staying with the pill, or like sticking with the pills. You know, it's fine. You don't want to have unprotected sex." In this framework, "unprotected sex" refers to sex unprotected from pregnancy—not sexually transmitted diseases. Her doctor explicitly communicated that her role would be to take birth control to protect herself from pregnancy when having condomless sex with her hypothetical prince charming. In light of her doctor's explicit gendering here, Gina's language around how she had never skipped birth control pills seems much less inconsequential. Indeed, she had never skipped taking pills because, in Gina's words, "Oh, no, no. I think I was a pretty good girl." Even when women tried to be "good girls" by consistently taking birth control to prevent pregnancy, however, gendered compulsory contraception could create challenges for their efforts—the next section shows how.

Compulsory Contraceptive Conundrums

As discussed briefly in the last section, the bifurcation of birth control into methods for women and methods for men—and the subsequent expectation that women would use methods designed for them—had negative consequences, not only for women's bodily autonomy, but also for their ability to meet their pregnancy prevention goals. For some women, widespread cultural expectations that couples need not use condoms in long-term relationships interacted with gender norms around contraception, putting them in complicated contraceptive double binds.[13]

Teresa (26 years old, Latina) recounted her experience getting pregnant while using the pill with her boyfriend, demonstrating the shortcomings of a model that holds that a partner's resistance to condom use is unproblematic so long as his partner uses female birth control:

> In the beginning, I was very very [wary] of doing anything without any type of protection, but then once I got on a birth control, we were still using protection but he was very insistent on not using the condom because he said it would feel better and because I don't know, I think I stupidly said, okay, fine, I gave in or something. So, towards the end we weren't using anything, I was just using birth control.

In explaining why condom use with her partner became a problem, Teresa said, "I think once I allowed him to [not wear a condom], he would just like shift and didn't want to. . . . I wasn't okay with it but I just knew the conflicts and I kind of gave in and yeah, so I hate that I do, then . . . I get pregnant but yeah." For Teresa, a combination of gender-related factors created challenges for her in preventing pregnancy. First, consistent with gendered expectations, she began using the pill to protect them from pregnancy after they became more serious. Second, like the women previously discussed, her partner began trying to avoid using condoms once pill use became an option. And, lastly, her partner had always been the one to provide the condoms, so his refusal to use a condom may not have entailed only refusing to use condoms in general but potentially may have also entailed his not bringing a condom at all. Although Teresa wanted to keep using condoms alongside the pill, which was particularly significant in terms of pregnancy prevention because she had trouble using the pill consistently, her partner's refusal to cooperate led them to use only her birth control, which resulted in a pregnancy.

Challenges with gendered compulsory contraception also occurred for women in casual relationships. Vanessa (22 years old, white) had been using the pill for several years before she experienced a pregnancy. Recall that Vanessa used condoms with her first partner and transitioned to the pill after her mother suggested that she start use and set up her doctor's appointment. She experienced a pregnancy with her third partner—a casual partner whom she would have sex with on the weekends. In describing how they discussed contraception, she said, "He brought it up. He wanted to make sure that I was on birth control and, you know, the whole like condom thing, like he didn't think that he had to use them if I was on birth control, which was, you know, I'm fine with that, I really don't care." So she said of their condom use, "If he had them, we used them, if he didn't, we didn't." She experienced a pregnancy because she skipped a couple of pills and they did not use condoms. Although she described her partner as being "really paranoid" about pregnancy, she also said he was comfortable not using condoms because he thought sex felt better without them and he assumed that her being "on the pill" was protection enough. Consistent with the experiences of other women with casual partners (and some women in serious relationships), the couple did not actually discuss whether she had indeed taken her pill consistently. Nonetheless, she reported that when she got pregnant, her partner did not appear entirely surprised:

> And I called him, I remember calling him, [I said] "I need to talk to you about something." And he was hot [angry], he was mad at me, he was like "oh, my God, I know what you're gonna say." . . . I'm like "What am I gonna say." And he was like "the pee thing." And I was like, "the pee thing," I was like I'm glad I'm dating a

[child] [laughter]. So he knew, like he knew, he said "I knew we shouldn't have made a mistake, like we should have used a condom." Oh, and there he went, all day.

Cases like Vanessa's and Teresa's help illuminate the experiences of some of the women for whom the pill was a less effective form of birth control. Vanessa, for example, had had trouble remembering to take her pill every day for years by the time she experienced a pregnancy. She had simply followed directions about how to "double-up" on missed pills. She had tried the patch because of her troubles with consistency but stopped using it because of news reports about the risk of adverse events. In her previous relationship, however, she and her partner had used condoms every time they had sex during the year that they dated. Thus, while Vanessa had actually had trouble taking the pill consistently in times past, she had a "backup" because her ex-boyfriend always wore a condom. This was not the case with the partner she had experienced a pregnancy with, however.

Unlike Teresa and Vanessa, who had already been using the pill when they stopped using condoms, other women began using prescription birth control because their partners would not cooperate with using condoms and their lack of condom use contributed to experiencing a pregnancy. Thus, contrary to assertions that transitioning from condoms to prescription birth control is the solution to condom resistance, these women's experiences show that such an approach can nonetheless fail to help women prevent pregnancy, even as it reifies them as responsible for doing so. Claire (20 years old, Asian), for example, discussed what she and her boyfriend did for birth control. In reflecting on her experiences with contraception, she said, "I just wished that I was more like anal about it. Like, 'Dude, no. You have to use a condom.' Or, 'I have to get on birth control or else we are not going to have sex.'" In addition to not having used anything for protection the first time she had intercourse with one of her boyfriends, Claire said, "We usually didn't [use contraception]. But I actually tried to go on the pill for three months but it wasn't reacting well to my body. So I switched over to the ring for a couple of months." While Claire liked the ring much better than the pill, she had trouble using it consistently because she could not afford to wait at the clinic and she had no means of transportation. Thus, she could get to a clinic only when friends could take her—a difficult proposition for some college students. Prescription birth control methods might not have been the best option for her at that point in her life, but she discussed one of the challenges to using condoms with her boyfriend (as an alternative to the pill or ring) later in the interview. She said, "I know [my boyfriend] refuses to use condoms. . . . He just doesn't like it. He'll go soft. Yeah. So it's not like he didn't want to. It's just that he couldn't and that would make me upset because it was like, 'Dude.'" Instead, if they were not using Claire's prescription birth control for coverage, they would use withdrawal or nothing. He ended up being unsupportive when he found out about the pregnancy.

As Claire alluded to in her comments about switching methods, preventing pregnancy became particularly challenging for women who felt dissatisfied with hormonal methods of birth control and preferred to use condoms. Cindy (20 years old, white) related experiencing a pregnancy with her boyfriend of three years because of inconsistent contraceptive use:

Um, I don't remember [if we used a condom at first sex] because me and him, I don't know. It was hella stupid but like we would always have sex without condoms and now I was trying to get him to wear them, now too. And he says like he doesn't like them. So honestly I don't think we ever used a condom. . . . [The first time] I didn't really think about it [having a condom]. Like with the other guys, like they always had it, you know. And like with him, I don't think he had it, so it just happened and like I really wanted to have sex with him, so . . . Yeah. And then like I don't know. I should be going to my doctor to get birth control but like I did take birth control for a little bit but it made me like hella fat, so. I don't want to take it even though I know I should.

Cindy had experienced two pregnancies with this partner, and she began using the pill after she became pregnant the first time. Her belief that she should begin using birth control again in part reflected gendered expectations of behavior more broadly, and in part was because, now that she "made" her boyfriend use a condom, they used them "100 percent of the time" but had sex less frequently. She said, "I bring it up all the time. He's like, 'We should have sex.' Or whatever, and I'm like, 'Yeah, if you put on a condom, then totally' but he's always like, 'No, I don't like how they feel.' Dah, dah, dah. 'It's constricting.' And I'm like, 'So?' I just tell him, 'Would you rather like have me be pregnant or you know, have sex?'" Experiences like Cindy's help illuminate the tradeoffs that women make in deciding *how* to contracept.

A critical analysis of Cindy's experience helps explain how those frameworks that treat condom resistance (regardless of gender) as unproblematic, because female partners can rely on prescription birth control, contribute to couples' having sex without contraception or to their using it inconsistently. In other words, because there is less accountability for male partners to wear condoms and the narrative remains that external condoms are a "male method," the onus is placed on women to use prescription birth control, have unprotected sex, or forego having sex altogether if they want to prevent pregnancy. In Cindy's case, she experienced each pregnancy during a time when she and her partner were not using any contraception. Women like Cindy often feel as though there are no good options. Indeed reflecting on her experience with contraception, she said, "Um, I don't know. It's not very satisfying but, there's like you want to have sex but you have to take something to not get pregnant. It kind of sucks. I've been meaning to go to my doctor but like instead I don't want to gain the weight. There's all these repercussions with everything you do." Indeed, Cindy felt as though she had to *take something* to prevent getting pregnant because her partner refused to *wear something* to avoid it.

As I show in the next section, assuming responsibility for preventing pregnancy using prescription birth control was not the only gendered constraint on the women's reproductive autonomy. Instead, they also faced a gendered responsibility to "take care of" a pregnancy when it occurred and social pressure to resolve the pregnancy in a particular way—whether by giving birth or by getting an abortion—that depended heavily on their social context.

Pregnancy Solutions and Gender-Foreclosed Resolutions

In this section, I focus not on whether pregnancy-resolution pathways were a choice or not for women but instead on elucidating the contours of their social contexts.[14] Thus, the analysis rests on the key reproductive justice premise that women's decisions can never be divorced from the public and political contexts in which they make them.[15] Nor can they be divorced from their relationship contexts and broader experiences with fertility.[16] As the women's stories demonstrated, they pursued particular pathways amid a gendered social politics that enabled and constrained their behaviors. While the majority of the chapter, then, has focused on the intersection of gender, contraception, and inequity preconception, this section shows how inequity in autonomy could play out after conception occurred.

Women had experiences with both casual and more serious partners assigning to them the responsibility for managing a potential conception. They faced these assumptions in varying contraceptive contexts—from those in which the concern revolved around a pregnancy that resulted from contraceptive failure to ones in which the couple did not contracept at all. Take, for example, Carolyn's (21 years old, white) description of an experience she had with a casual partner whom she met at a party on the last night of a trip abroad:

> And he helped me pack up my stuff and then we went to his bed because he had a bottom bunk and I had a top bunk. And we had sex and it was horrible. It was absolutely horrible and he didn't have a condom and I didn't have a condom and it was like, "It's fine. I'll just pull out." And I was really drunk and I was like, "I don't think that's a good idea." But I said fine. . . . And he didn't pull out in time and I was, and he came in like a couple minutes and he's like, "This never happens to me. This never happens to me." And like making this big macho deal and I was like, "Excuse me. I don't really give a shit about your manliness right now. You might have just gotten me pregnant. So I don't like you right now."

While neither Carolyn nor her partner had discussed pregnancy before their sexual encounter, she recalled that he had asked her if she were "pro-life" or "pro-choice" after they had sex, when she began getting "all of his information" because of the failed withdrawal. Interestingly, while her partner did not explicitly state what he would prefer that she do, he did make it clear that she was ultimately responsible for doing *something*. And, in fact, when the interviewer asked if they had talked about having a child before they had intercourse, she said, "No. [After sex] he actually said, 'Yeah, you're gonna get it taken care of, right?' And I was like, 'Yeah.' So the exact opposite." While her partner may not have simply assumed that she was using prescription contraception, the operating assumption was nonetheless a gendered one. Carolyn's experience teaches a broader lesson about the social expectations that women face when navigating sex and contraception. In the event of a breakdown in the gender-normative script that "men bring condoms and women take pills," the focus may shift from prevention to what happens after conception, at which point another gendered pathway emerges. In both preventing pregnancy and dealing with it, then, women are expected to figure out how to "take care of" the situation.

Sometimes women faced assumptions that birth was the "right" way to get a pregnancy "taken care of," owing both to gender-normative expectations of motherhood for women and to partner preferences for pregnancy resolution. Desiree (21 years old, Black) had to grapple with a particularly challenging partner, whom she met while she was studying abroad. When discussing her experiences contracepting and eventually getting pregnant with him, she said, "Yeah, in the beginning we used condoms and then after a while we stopped using anything . . . after like a month and a half . . . we stopped using contraception. . . . Like I said, he didn't like to use them [condoms] because like it hurt him. . . . It was hard to get him to wear condoms. . . . I would get mad but I just stayed with him. It's my fault [that the pregnancy occurred]." Like the women discussed earlier in this chapter, Desiree assumed responsibility for becoming pregnant even though her partner did not cooperate with her efforts to prevent pregnancy. Despite his noncooperation, he nonetheless tried to constrain her choices around how she should resolve a pregnancy should they conceive. She said, "He was trying to convince me to not get an abortion if I ever did get pregnant. . . . Yeah, I told him I didn't know what I would do." When she did get pregnant with him, however, she felt that she was fairly clear about her preferences. She said, "Yeah. I was thinking in the back of my mind abortion. That's how my mom raised me to be practical and like be reasonable." While Desiree felt as though she wanted to get an abortion, her boyfriend tried to get her to carry the pregnancy to term. She recalled his reaction to her pregnancy, saying, "But he was like 'Listen, if you will have an abortion, I will not talk to you ever again.' He found ways to make me feel so bad about it. . . . He said he wouldn't talk to me anymore and his family too. . . . But they said, 'There's always a way, Desiree. If you had the kid, there would always be a way.'" Desiree, as a result, had to contend with both her partner's and his family's beliefs about how she should resolve the pregnancy. Her experience demonstrates how women could feel alienated from loved ones who tried to limit their options for pregnancy. This was particularly significant for Desiree because she became pregnant while in a foreign country and had no relatives of her own, but just her boyfriend and his family, to support her. Rather than providing her with the support that she needed, her boyfriend (and his family) pressured her to pursue birth—even though he knew *pre-conception* that she would consider abortion and even though his own refusal to use condoms despite her protests contributed to the pregnancy.

Even when loved ones did not talk with participants about how to prevent pregnancy, they might nonetheless still have communicated to women that they would be responsible for resolving the pregnancy in a particular way. Whereas birth was considered by her boyfriend and his family to be the right option for Desiree, whose mother did not talk with her about contraception before she became sexually active, abortion was considered the right option for Marie (21 years old, white). Marie recalled how she learned about birth control in her sex education class. The only conversation that she had with a parent about contraception involved one about the pill with her father, which took place during a discussion that did not actually focus on the pill as a method of birth control. She said, "My dad did say to me that birth control regulates your cycle and it makes your boobs bigger. He's like, 'Oh, if you want bigger boobs, just start birth control.' He's a sexist kind of guy. But um, yeah, it was just through that. I never really had any kind of conversation about sex or being a woman with my mom really." Although she never discussed contraceptive methods as a way to prevent pregnancy with her parents, her father did talk with her about abortion. When talking about her parents' views during a conversation about what Marie would have done in the event of a hypothetical pregnancy with one of her partners, for example, Marie said, "Uh, I would have probably just gotten an abortion. It was also during high school, at the time, my dad had just came out and said, 'If anything happens, if you get pregnant, let me know. We'll get the operation done.'" Experiences like Marie's illustrate in clear terms how gendered expectations shaped decision making—although her parents talked with her about neither contraception nor abortion, they made it clear who would define the appropriate course of action were a pregnancy to occur. It would not be Marie.

Women's narratives about pregnancy with their partners demonstrated the importance of a nuanced analysis that situates their gendered reproductive experiences in social context. For the women in my study, their partners' and families' perceptions of what the "right" pregnancy outcome was, for example, could depend on age, the status of a relationship, and the couple's financial circumstances. For women like Holly (the 20-year-old white woman whose partner called her a bitch for not resuming pill use), the assumption that she should consider her partner's preferences remained, but the "right" outcome for a potential pregnancy was not considered a birth. Holly not only had problems getting her boyfriend to wear a condom; she also had to contend with assumptions about pregnancy resolution that did not align with her own preferences about how to manage her fertility. She said the following about whether she had ever thought that she would have children with him:

Um, I thought I was too young. I thought, like, [he] would have been a good dad, but he was way too immature at that time. He had in his head that if I got pregnant, I'd have an abortion because we were so young and I'm not really comfortable with that. . . . So it was like this big tiff that we would have because I never got pregnant, but we'd have pregnancy scares or something, or my period was late and stuff like that. And he would always just be like, "Well, if you're pregnant, we'll just go to the clinic." And I'm like, "It's not that simple. It means a lot more to me than just making a doctor's appointment and getting this taken care of." So because he was like that, I was kind of like, I don't think that we'll ever actually have kids.

Her boyfriend may have felt particularly comfortable pressuring her to have sex without a condom (as discussed previously) because he believed, in the event of a pregnancy, she would resolve it in the way that he preferred. Thus, Holly's challenges with gendered compulsory birth control with this partner involved not only his attempts to constrain her contraceptive choices but also his perceived right to constrain her pregnancy choices.

While a pregnancy can end in numerous ways—birth, abortion, adoption, or miscarriage—the very few women in the study who considered adoption faced challenges to their autonomy in pursuing that outcome. Claire, the 20-year-old Asian woman who had trouble getting her boyfriend to wear condoms and as a result tried various prescription methods, described what happened when she became pregnant with him. She recounted how she and her boyfriend were not on the same page about adoption. When asked if she considered abortion and adoption, she replied, "I did [consider adoption]. But he didn't even ask me. He was like, 'How do you want me to help you get an abortion?' like that. Yeah, so I was like, 'Dude, what if I wanted to have it?' and he was like, 'There's no way you can have it.'" Particularly challenging for Claire was her boyfriend's immediate assumption that she would have an abortion, which he expressed as soon as she returned to the car from the health clinic and delivered the news that she was pregnant. She said, "[he] is a very, very, very calculating, meticulous guy. And so when I told him, he was sad but he just put off his feelings to think about, 'Oh, what are the next steps? How can we fix this problem?'"

Indeed, when she expressed how it hurt her that he did not seem fazed by how upset she was, she recalled his saying, "'What do you want me to do?' And blah, blah, blah, 'Do you just want to sit here and cry all freaking day? Or do you want to try to solve this?'"

Although Claire recalled that her boyfriend was "meticulous" and "calculating," it appears as if he were meticulous and calculating in devising a plan to help her *resolve* the pregnancy in the way that he wished but not necessarily in supporting her plan to prevent one. As discussed previously, he often made it difficult for them to prevent pregnancy by refusing to wear condoms, even when he knew pregnancy was possible. In fact, he also did little to support her efforts to use prescription contraception. Claire faced multiple threats to her reproductive freedom: she had a partner who refused to wear condoms and made it difficult for her not to resort to prescription birth control even though she had trouble using it. When a pregnancy occurred, however, her partner was not equally uninvolved in decision making. In the end, just as partners could limit women's autonomy in choosing a contraceptive method, they could also do so when a pregnancy occurred—by constraining decisions about birth, abortion, and adoption.

JUST GET ON THE . . . IUD?

Authors often remark that writing a book provides an interesting lesson in self-reflection. Completing this book proved no exception. It was only after analyzing the data and fleshing out my discussion of my own contraceptive trajectory that I realized my experience getting an IUD might, in fact, be an example of gendered compulsory contraception. After all, my doctor did not encourage me to continue using condoms (perhaps because the

IUD is so effective at preventing pregnancy) and my partner and I did immediately stop using condoms after I got it. While I do not have any experience with pregnancy, my experiential knowledge of the IUD did allow me to see how the very women being channeled into taking primary responsibility for preventing births might also take for granted that doing so was entirely unproblematic. That is the power of the Black feminist way of knowing that I deploy in this book. It is a way of knowing that forced me to subject my own experience to critical analysis. In so doing, it helped me see how even people well-informed about gender might consent to participate in a gendered compulsory birth control system that reproduced gender inequity in their relationships and could present challenges to their reproductive autonomy. That is, it gave me insight into how people might buy into dominant cultural practices, even as those practices contribute to their subordination—what social scientists refer to as *hegemony.*[17] For years, I thought nothing of taking primary responsibility for pregnancy prevention, even when the method that I was supposed to be able to "set and forget" produced intense cramps, more frequent periods, and "spotting" *every day* for the first year (of five) that I had it. That, I finally, truly understood, was the power of hegemony. It took me only fifteen years of distance from reading about the concept for the first time in college and five years of one-sided, but consensual, gendered labor preventing pregnancy to finally get it.

4 Selective Selection

Myths are more than made-up stories. They are also firmly held beliefs that represent and attempt to explain what we perceive to be the truth. They can become more credible than reality, holding fast even in the face of airtight statistics and rational argument to the contrary.

DOROTHY ROBERTS, *Killing the Black Body*

In Dorothy Roberts's canonical book on race and reproduction, Roberts discusses how racial stereotypes shape a powerful focus on regulating Black women's fertility in the United States. She elaborates on how racist notions of Black women's degeneracy, immorality, and neglectfulness as mothers have led to policies and practices that subjugate Black women and deprive them of reproductive freedom. Davis's work on medical racism and premature birth among Black women demonstrates how these ideas continue to shape outcomes today.[1] Gendered expectations of behavior have particularly important consequences for the reproductive autonomy of Black women and other marginalized women against this backdrop. Frameworks that largely ignore gender, however, may render the strategies that diverse women use to navigate contraceptive inequality invisible. It is these strategies that I uncovered as a result of carefully listening to women's voices. I elucidate them in the pages that follow.

In this chapter, I focus on the fifty women who had experienced a pregnancy to demonstrate how broader patterns of unchecked gender inequality—not "careless" contraceptive behavior—limited women's ability to prevent pregnancy and control their fertility on their own terms. Four women were Asian, twenty-three were Black, six were Latina, and seventeen were white. The analysis shows that, while almost all women had experienced a pregnancy that they would call "unplanned," women's contraceptive contexts differed by race. White and Asian women were more likely to have followed the traditional gendered script in contraception that I described previously, wherein couples transitioned from using condoms to using highly effective methods designed for women over the course of their relationships. Black and Latina women, on the other hand, were less likely to follow this trajectory. Thus, while white and Asian women were more likely to have experienced a pregnancy as a result of inconsistently using a prescription birth control method, Black and Latina women were more likely to have conceived because of inconsistent use of condoms. Whereas the previous chapters focused more heavily on gender-normative behavior, this chapter focuses on elucidating the social contexts in which women engaged in non-normative behavior. The nine non-Black women who did not conform to the traditional gendered script tended to be from less privileged backgrounds. The seventeen Black women who violated norms also tended to come from disadvantaged backgrounds, though there were several who were more privileged. Recall that all women had experienced a pregnancy. While less advantaged women as a whole may have been more likely to resist gendered expectations of contraceptive responsibility, therefore, their more advantaged counterparts who acquiesced did not "escape" pregnancy by conforming to gender norms. Instead, the blame may have shifted more heavily to them because they imperfectly used "their" prescription birth control method.

As I show, understanding the context in which women resist prescription birth control use—especially when faced with partners who will not cooperate with condoms—is crucial for disrupting narratives that position women, especially Black women, as irrational for foregoing contraception when they do not desire a pregnancy. It reveals the importance of using an interdisciplinary lens to study health behaviors and make recommendations, instead of pursuing a long-standing public health approach that single-mindedly promotes prescription birth control for the women most "at risk" of pregnancy. This approach may encroach on their reproductive autonomy even as it fails to help them prevent pregnancy. The lens that I advocate focuses on the broader *social conditions* that shape pregnancy,[2] rather than on the causes (like improving birth control use) that public health proponents pursue as the factors most closely related to pregnancy in what social scientists refer to as the "causal chain." Simply trying to get more women to conform to gender expectations dictating they use prescription birth control to prevent pregnancy does little to nothing to improve the social contexts that make it difficult for them to use these methods as they would like. The intersectional gender analysis that I offer here, on the other hand, provides insight into concrete strategies that can positively transform women's sexual and reproductive experiences. I show that interrupting the perpetuation of gendered compulsory birth control is crucial for this transformation.

A key idea in gender theory is that gender is a social accomplishment that is fundamentally achieved through interaction.[3] People thus earn their positions in particular gender categories by interacting in culturally approved ways—wearing gender-appropriate clothes, expressing emotions in gender-appropriate ways, and so on.

From an intersectional perspective, race and gender shape each other as systems that organize difference,[4] from the individual level at which people interact to the social structural level at which policies govern large institutions. While dominant gender norms and beliefs are widely understood and enforced by people in society, subgroups can also hold beliefs that go against dominant ones—what are known as "counterhegemonic beliefs." These beliefs can contribute to "undoing gender"—reducing gender differences rather than perpetually re-creating them.[5]

The number of studies focusing on how race shapes resistance to gender is extremely limited. The research that does exist suggests racial differences in historical attitudes about gender. Take the subgroup differences in gender beliefs about paid work, for example. Blacks have historically held much more positive beliefs about Black women's education and paid work than whites have about white women's education and paid work.[6] Despite the lack of acknowledgment of their experience in the broader discourse on work, Black women in the United States have also always been more likely to work than white women—whether owing to oppression when they were enslaved or because they sought compensation as employees.[7] The histories are similar for other women of color, immigrant women, and poor women, reflecting the role of economic necessity in shaping practices and broader beliefs about gender and work. Thus, the prevalence of counterhegemonic beliefs matters for the organization of society because people's behavior is at least partially influenced by the ideologies that they subscribe to, which as earlier chapters have shown, are at least partially based on their social context. Following history's lead suggests the importance of going beneath the surface of taken-for-granted behaviors to examine how counterhegemonic beliefs and practices may exist alongside dominant ones. As I show in the following sections, Black women's non-normative behavior undermined gender in their relationships, even as these same behaviors might also have resulted in pregnancy.

"SO I WAS LIKE, WHATEVER SIZE YOU NEED"

Contrary to gender expectations derived from the "his condom/her birth control" framework, Black women were more likely to bring their own condoms than were women of other races. This finding held whether I was examining the sample of women who had experienced a pregnancy, as discussed in this chapter, or the experiences of the full sample of women. Whereas no more than half of Asian, Latina, or white women who had experienced a pregnancy had ever brought their own condoms, almost three-quarters (70%) of Black women had ever done so.

Providing condoms was largely unremarkable for many Black women. Tiana (21 years old, Black), for example, described one of many experiences providing condoms during a casual sexual encounter: "I had it. He had, 'cause I had a heart shaped [box], that was supposed to be my sorority pin box, full of condoms. So I was like, whatever size you need. So I was like, whatever. So, yeah."

Unlike the handful of women of other races who had provided condoms and then discovered that they were apparently too small for their partners only during the encounter, Tiana not only had an ample supply of condoms but was also prepared with different sizes to ensure her partner had a variety to choose from. Her decision to tell him "whatever size you need" further underscored her comfort around condom use and her sexuality, clearly indicating to her partner that he was one of many men with whom she could have sex.

For other women, bringing condoms reflected their own unique needs. Marion (22 years old, Black) had a latex allergy. Rather than resorting to prescription birth control, Marion simply made sure to carry her own condoms. When discussing condom provision in one of her recent relationships, Marion said, "I did [provide them]. And pretty much now I provide condoms all the time because I need polyurethane. . . . It's Trojan Supra is what I use but it's polyurethane. It's not latex. . . . So it's thinner but it's just as reliable as latex, but it doesn't give me infections. . . . The only thing is they're slightly more expensive than regular condoms though." Marion learned she had an allergy only after getting infections from intercourse with latex condoms. To ensure that she could use condoms moving forward, she sacrificed her limited financial resources to buy more expensive ones. In fact, Marion was comfortable asserting that her partners use condoms, whether she brought her own condoms or not. When discussing sex with a previous partner, who knew she was pregnant, for example, Marion said he had told her, "You can't get pregnant" after she asked him if he had a condom. She responded humorously, "Obviously nigga, but you got some condoms?" Rather than trying to negotiate with her partner over condom use, Marion confidently asserted that he should wear a condom—whether or not he had intended to and whether or not she could get pregnant.

For other women, their comfort with getting and using condoms proved particularly useful during encounters in which they faced partners who were unprepared or made excuses to facilitate having condomless sex. Malia (22 years old, Black) described how she handled a situation in which neither she nor her partner had a condom. When the interviewer asked if she had used condoms with her partner, she said, "Oh yeah, the whole nine yards. . . . It was just like, um, do you have a condom? Oh you don't have one? Okay, let's go get one. And we'll come back and finish what we started." As discussed previously, some women (including Black women) had sex without a condom when none were available, but Black women differed markedly in being comfortable with buying condoms in the event that their partners had not done so or refused to. Recall the experience of Sharon (24 years old, Black) in chapter 1, for example, who bought condoms for her and her partner because she remarked that he was too much of "a fuckin sissy" to do it himself.

That women were willing to go against gender norms to provide their own condoms did not mean it was always easy to sustain the behavior over long periods of time. Sonia (20 years old, white and Latina) was one of the few non-Black women in the subsample who went against gender norms by both providing her own condoms and extensively researching withdrawal (understood as a "male method"). She and her partner eventually stopped using condoms nonetheless. Of her experience with her long-term boyfriend, Sonia said, "Like we talked about maybe changing brands [because of irritation with spermicide] or using a different kind or sometimes he would not have one on him, and I would go buy them before I went to go see him." Eventually, they transitioned to using withdrawal because she could not always afford to buy condoms, and "he would just make excuses like, 'Oh, it's kind of far to walk. Do you really just want to wait here while I go buy condoms?' And like, 'Well, okay.'" Although she had experienced a pregnancy and had had an abortion a year into the relationship, she still preferred not to begin using hormonal birth control and felt "torn" about continuing to use pullout. They continued using withdrawal for more than two years after her initial pregnancy. Though her comfort with using withdrawal as a primary birth control method is inconsistent with recommendations that women use more effective contraception, using withdrawal made sense to her because she had not become pregnant again, did not want to begin using prescription birth control, and attributed her first pregnancy to her partner not withdrawing in time. Indeed, when discussing whether or not he was good at withdrawing, she recalled a couple of instances in which he said, "That was weird. I felt like I just had an orgasm." So it is likely that he not only failed to use the method correctly but also failed to be forthcoming with her about his inability to do so. As a consequence, she was not comfortable with a wholesale rejection of withdrawal, especially when she was less interested in other options. Refusing to begin prescription birth control when partners rejected condoms was one of the patterns that distinguished Sonia (and other women in this chapter) from their counterparts of other races who had experienced a pregnancy.

"I WAS NEVER TOO KEEN ON ALL THE BIRTH CONTROL STUFF"

Nationally representative data show that while Black and Latina women are less likely to have used the pill and more likely to have used the shot than white women, more than three-quarters of women from each group have used some sort of hormonal method (86% of Black women, 81% of Latina women, and 91% of white women).[8] Black and Latina women are less likely to be consistent users of birth control than white women, however.[9] Black women are also more likely to be nonusers of contraception than white women.[10] The following section underscores a key insight from the broader literature: the effectiveness of contraceptive methods is only one factor that women weigh in deciding whether to begin prescription birth control.[11]

Rather than following the traditional gender division of labor in contraception, according to which women began using a prescription method after couples had transitioned into long-term sexual relationships, Black women continued to expect their partners to wear condoms. They did not generally feel as though they "should" begin using hormonal birth control. As couples did not always use condoms, however, this could lead to unprotected sex.

Consistent with expectations from the literature showing that most Black women have used a hormonal form of contraception at some point, a majority of Black women in the study had done so before they experienced a pregnancy. Thus, their experiences in getting pregnant were usually not a result of their never having used a highly effective method. Instead, many simply did not believe that they had to use prescription birth control to avoid pregnancy, or they did not believe the couple's contraceptive regimen should depend solely on the woman's use of a prescription method. Shanice (27 years old, Black), for example, had used the pill in a previous relationship, but she had more trouble doing so with a subsequent partner. In an earlier relationship, she and her partner had both bought their own condoms and they had always used them, even though she was also on the pill. She talked with the interviewer about her challenges with a later partner:

> INTERVIEWER: So that first time with him what—did you guys use a condom?
>
> SHANICE: We used a condom the first time. We got careless around maybe around three months after having sex. And that's when I got pregnant.
>
> INTERVIEWER: Ok so then that was maybe like five months after you guys started seeing each other.
>
> SHANICE: Yeah
>
> INTERVIEWER: So were you on the pill at that time?
>
> SHANICE: No. I was actually on the patch I believe. I had the patch. But I remember I took the patch off because it started to—it like burned my skin.
>
> INTERVIEWER: Oh my gosh
>
> SHANICE: It left a burn mark so I remember taking it off and I was supposed to start a different method and it just wasn't a priority to me at the time.
>
> INTERVIEWER: So like it was one of those in-between times?
>
> SHANICE: Yeah. I was transitioning because I was going to go with the Depo shot but then I didn't know about the shot so I was like, "I don't know, I'm kind of scared to get that," and he just didn't want to wear a condom.
>
> INTERVIEWER: Oh he didn't.
>
> SHANICE: That was just rude.

Key to Shanice's understanding of her experience was the belief that it was not solely her responsibility to prevent pregnancy. Like many women, she faced a partner who would not wear a condom, but she did not take one of the gendered paths of least resistance—prioritizing prescription birth control. She did not believe that she "had" to begin using the shot or any other prescription method immediately because her partner would not cooperate with using condoms. She also did not believe she had to "bite the bullet" and use a method that she was not comfortable with. She accepted responsibility for the pregnancy, saying "we got careless," but also noted her partner's culpability and disregard for her wishes by commenting on his rudeness for refusing to wear a condom.

For other Black women, the notion that they should transition onto a prescription birth control method after being in a long-term relationship was itself incongruous with their own beliefs and behaviors. Believing that condom use was an important component of their protection strategy, rather than being something just for men, was central to their understandings. Maya (23 years old, Black), for example, discussed using condoms the first time that she had sex. After the interviewer asked her if she was concerned about pregnancy, she said, "No, not at that time. Not at the time. I think I trust[ed] him a lot. He was my boyfriend at the time. . . . Plus I used protection. So that was the main thing. I told myself if I was ever going to do it before I got married, if I have sex with anyone, I have to put on a condom 'cause, man, I can't do it." Later, in a four-year-long relationship, however, Maya relied on withdrawal for eight months before she ended up conceiving. She tried the pill after the birth of her son at the suggestion of her medical provider but stopped because she could not remember to take it every day. She eventually got an IUD after a second pregnancy with this partner. Upon reflecting on her experiences and any times that she wished she had used birth control, however, she never expressed dissatisfaction with not having used prescription contraception earlier, even though she was satisfied with the IUD and regretted having her son because she had wanted to wait until after marriage to have children. She used prescription contraception sporadically, therefore, but did not see it as an absolutely necessary part of her contraceptive repertoire.

Women like Tabitha (23 years old, Black) made this even more explicit. Tabitha had experience bringing her own condoms—including one instance in which she took a package full of condoms when she flew at least six thousand miles to visit her boyfriend because condoms were so expensive in the country she was visiting. She discussed her feelings on using prescription birth control, saying that, in addition to feeling uncomfortable with the side effects,

> For [me], if you're in a committed relationship, because condoms are about 99 percent effective if used correctly, so it's like, using condoms and birth control, there's no point. But, if you're in a long-term relationship or if you both agree to stop using, you should be on birth control. But yeah, so that's my thinking. It's kind of like putting on two seat belts when you get in a car crash. Two seat belts aren't going to save you; one will be just fine.

Tabitha had used the patch in the past but did not want to resume using prescription birth control again. Though her approximation of condom efficacy was nearly spot-on (they are 98 percent effective when used consistently and correctly), the challenge that Tabitha faced was that her boyfriend refused to use condoms. Indeed, in discussing what happened when she brought condoms from the United States, she said, "Then I brought them out and I was like, 'This is your gift' and he just ripped it open [the wrapping] and he threw it away. I was like, 'Okay, whatever.' . . . He just threw it back on the bed like, 'What is this?'" They used withdrawal instead and she experienced a pregnancy. Although some interpretations of her behavior might suggest that she was simply being careless for using withdrawal or not transitioning onto a prescription birth control method, her discussion at the end of the interview demonstrated the importance of considering other potential explanations. When talking about whether or not she felt satisfied with contraception, for example, she said, "I just wish there were male birth control. Because I just feel like, why should the woman always have to like, take the pill, the Ring, the patch, you know, like, the IUD, why should we always have to go through this and they do absolutely nothing?" Tabitha's condom choice would have made it impossible for her partner to do "nothing" had everything gone to plan. Instead, her partner's rejection undermined her birth control decision and she agreed to withdrawal.

As several of these women's narratives highlight, Black women often refused to accept primary responsibility for preventing pregnancy—that is, they not only refused to begin prescription birth control as a "natural" progression of the relationship after being with partners for several months but also refused to begin using it when faced with partners who did not want to wear condoms. When discussing her preference for condoms over prescription birth control, for example, Kiara (27 years old, Black) said,

> I never was too keen on like on all the birth control stuff like that. . . . I've always been a naturalist kind of person. So I don't take too many pills. I don't eat red meat. I'm one of those type of people. . . . And I was always worried about side effects and I always knew that I was always pretty much sexually healthy, which

mean I don't want to expose myself, my mother always worked at Kaiser. I was always exposed to the ills of STDs and safe sex practices. So I've always been pretty much safe sexually.

Several women in the sample worried about side effects or did not feel particularly "keen" on using prescription birth control, as discussed in chapter 2. Unlike Kiara, however, many of them used it nonetheless. Since Kiara felt comfortable using condoms and did not intend to stop using them, she did not believe that it was necessary to go against her self-described "naturalist" tendencies and begin using prescription birth control. Indeed, implicit in her discussion of having safe sex was the assumption that beginning prescription birth control meant stopping condom use, something that she was opposed to. Although at age 14 Kiara had used condoms inconsistently with one boyfriend (which resulted in a pregnancy), she used condoms consistently every time thereafter, including during a ten-year relationship, during which the couple stopped using condoms only because they were ready to have a child together. At the time of the interview, she continued to use condoms, refusing to begin using prescription birth control even when facing challenging partners. Of using condoms with one boyfriend whom she dated for a year, she said, "We used protection [condoms] all the time. He didn't want to. That's another thing about the dating now. The guys don't want to use condoms now. . . . They don't say anything. . . . They just try to keep everything going without and a couple of guys . . . I feel like they tried to slip the condoms off." Kiara was able to get her boyfriend to wear condoms despite his protests. When partners gave her trouble, she said, "I'd get up and say, 'You have to go.' I've never been one to mince words if it's something that I'm not feeling." Of course, as discussed, not every woman had as much success getting partners to wear condoms (or felt comfortable refusing sex if their partners rejected them), which resulted in unprotected sex for some of them.

Although I focus largely on Black women in this chapter, there were instances when white women and others demonstrated similar non-normative behaviors. Denise (25 years old, white), for example, brought her own condoms and decided not to rely primarily on prescription contraception after she grew weary of hormones. In this lengthy exchange with an interviewer, she explained how she decided to stop using prescription birth control altogether after taking Plan B twice, and how the couple eventually started having unprotected sex:

> DENISE: Right, and I was just like "oh, my God, what am I doing to my body, like you know, I have so many hormones in me right now." Plus I was not, I was just not being consistent with my pill at all so I was just like I need to not be on it right now and let my body clean itself out.
>
> INTERVIEWER: Mm, hmm.
>
> DENISE: Of course, you know, being in a long-term relationship that's not exactly the best time to be doing it [stopping prescription birth control], but you know, we sort of decided that like we would go by my cycle and have sex with a condom, you know, up until—we could have sex without a condom for like the first week like just after my period and then for the following two weeks, you know, have sex with a condom, and could only do it with a condom.
>
> INTERVIEWER: Yeah, mm, hmm.
>
> DENISE: And then after that do it without a condom again. And it was just a cusp day and I knew it, you know, and the whole

time that like we were having sex I just kept, I kept feeling, I kept thinking like Denise, say something, Denise, say something. But we had had, I had said something previously, like one other time, and he was almost hurt. He felt like I didn't trust him.

INTERVIEWER: Oh, so you felt . . .

DENISE: And so it, you know, it made me sort of bite my tongue back because I was confident—not confident but I felt that he knew it [was a cusp day] and it was just me being paranoid, you know. And then it happened [I got pregnant] and I was just like "OH, MY GOD, WHAT DID YOU DO?" I blamed him for a really long time.

Thus, even though Denise's partner likely knew that they needed to use condoms to protect the couple from pregnancy, Denise was hesitant to raise the issue because doing so previously had generated conflict. Consistent with the experiences of the many Black women whom I describe in this chapter, however, Denise did not blame herself for not preventing the pregnancy using prescription birth control. Indeed, she blamed her partner for not wearing a condom and getting her pregnant. While one might argue that it is inconsistent to suggest that it was fair for Denise to require her partner to wear a condom (a "male" method) but unfair for partners to require women to use prescription birth control (a "female" method), recall that my argument is that condoms should not be understood in a sexed or gendered way in the first place. They interact with both people's bodies and, thus, need not be understood as "belonging" solely to men.

For other women, who resisted gendered expectations, their reluctance did not stem from a distrust of hormones. They simply did not prioritize hormonal methods for their contraceptive effects or were uninterested in changing behaviors that were incompatible with pill use. Jayla (21 years old, Black), was willing to use the pill to regulate her period but did not feel that she needed to begin using it to protect herself from pregnancy. In fact, she had never used the pill during times when she could become pregnant. Of her experience using it, she said, "Um, I took it. . . . I wasn't sexually active at the time, I took it because my periods are very painful. So they worked wonders for my period. And it was like about right at the time that I ran out they were like a month or two after is when I started having sex. 'Cause like I took it when I first left for college." Although she considered refilling her prescription, she explained that "Because I smoked, I was afraid that it would give me a stroke or something like that. So I wasn't in a big rush." When asked what she planned to do for contraception in the future, she replied she would use "pills and condoms," saying, "Hopefully by that time. I mean, I can't—I can't say because I do wanna be with someone right now. I wanna have sex . . . so . . . um, hopefully by that time I'll quit smoking so I would definitely do the pill again. 'Cause I don't see my period changing any time soon. It worked wonders." Even when discussing using the pill for contraception, then, her attention remained focused on how the pill could help alleviate the cramps that she experienced with her period.

Jayla's experience also demonstrated the challenges that some women had while relying on condoms, which made them firm believers in using at least two methods of birth control. Though she did not want to stop smoking, she kept the pill on her radar because the one pregnancy that she experienced was a consequence of condom failure. As a result, she said, "I wish that I woulda been on the pill with my daughter's dad. And it's touchy 'cause I do love my daughter." Though she carried the pregnancy to term, and loved her daughter, her experience getting pregnant even though she used a condom every time with that partner had made her consider using both condoms and the pill. Her desire to use dual methods, rather than just the pill, was consistent with data showing Black women are more likely than white women to use both condoms and hormonal methods than they are to use hormonal methods alone.[12]

Adrianna (29 years old, Black), who used condoms with her partner even after a tubal ligation, also believed in the importance of using two methods. Adrianna's story, perhaps more than any other woman's narrative in this entire book, demonstrated the importance of critically examining women's attitudes and experiences to understand the circumstances that contribute to their experiences with pregnancy. Her experiences with conception resulted from a number of factors, only one of which was her non-normative behavior. She believed women should use prescription birth control and condoms because of her own experiences getting pregnant, once because of a sexual assault, during which her rapist did not use a condom, and later with a partner who did use a condom. Because of these experiences, when talking about her first experience having sex at fifteen, Adrianna said,

Yeah, you need to wait. If you can't wait, you better get you some protection and not some old junky protection. I don't care if he is using a rubber. It's protecting you guys from diseases and it's protecting you from getting pregnant. But sometimes that don't work and boys are slick. They'll tell you they got it on and they don't have it on. So if you're gonna be having sex, you better get yourself some contraceptives for yourself.

Her tubal ligation was in response to her desire not to have any kids with her partner, whom she believed was a bad father and who "might try and make [her] pregnant" if they relied only on condoms. This framework, one that suggests that two methods be used rather than only one (prescription birth control), contributes to undoing gender in relationships by holding both partners accountable for preventing pregnancy, even when the woman's prescription birth control would provide effective coverage.

Adrianna was also one of the only women in the sample to explicitly discuss the intersection of contraception and gendered violence, pushing back against assertions that women should automatically use prescription birth control to prevent pregnancy. Although other women discussed the unfairness of requiring that women be responsible for using prescription birth control, Adrianna questioned the very structure of prescription birth control use and how women receive services, situating the experience in a larger context involving power, disadvantage, and violence. When asked whether she had any suggestions for making it easier for women to get birth control when they wanted to, Adrianna redirected the question:

It is [easy to get birth control]. But, if I was giving out birth control, I know Planned Parenthood probably have you fill out a little survey and all that stuff. I think you really need to talk with these people that are coming to get birth control, you know. Because just handing it out to them, "Here, use this. You won't get pregnant." Man, what is that doing? "Okay, here. Go have all the sex you want, but don't get pregnant." I really think that they need to be counseled before you give them any birth control. You need to know why this 12-year-old is sitting here asking for birth control. Okay, she's sexually active. With who? You know? Is she sexually active with someone in her family? Is she sexually active with her step-dad or is she sexually active with her boyfriend? And then okay, boyfriend? How old is her boyfriend? You know what I'm saying? So if I was, if I had control over that, no, to get this birth control, you have to come in my office and you have to sit down and you have to talk. I need to know why you want this birth control. I need to know who is your partner. I need to know why are you having sex so young.

Although access to contraception is important for women's repro-ductive autonomy, Adrianna presented a critique of traditional approaches to prescription birth control for women that ignore social location. Although her remarks may be read as intrusive because of the amount of information that she suggests providers gather, they nonetheless integrate a reproductive justice frame-work. This framework considers women's social context and chal-lenges the notion that using prescription birth control is always an autonomous decision. For example, being forced to use prescription birth control to hide familial sexual abuse may prevent pregnancy (a health outcome), but it would be part of a larger attack on a wom-an's reproductive and bodily autonomy. Thus, Adrianna's com-ments highlight the importance of avoiding a focus on pregnancy prevention as the single most important issue at stake in women's use of prescription birth control. Instead, researchers and practi-tioners must consider the social contexts in which women reside.

There are those who might suggest that Black and marginalized women in the study were less likely to use birth control, not because they were particularly committed to resisting gender, but because "unplanned pregnancy" is less "consequential" for Black and less advantaged women or because their communities are somehow more accepting of unplanned pregnancies. According to this argument, even if marginalized women's behavior *contributes* to reducing gender inequality in contraception, a desire to reduce this inequality is not its primary *cause*; a lack of motivation to prevent pregnancy is. To them, I first say that marginalized people's right to reproductive freedom is inalienable. Their reasons for exercising their right to assert bodily autonomy and resist forces that would render them primary contraceptors are irrelevant. Even bracketing their right to reproductive freedom, however, it is a widely accepted logical fallacy to posit that people do not really want to avoid pregnancy if they fail to use birth control. Such an argument assumes that using birth control is a sign of motivation to avoid pregnancy and then cites lack of use as evidence for lack of motivation. There is a simple and logically valid way to settle this question: turning to the data. I find it unsurprising that the data do not support this argument. The women in the sample did not use birth control at times when they wanted to avoid pregnancy (and some had an abortion when a pregnancy occurred), and they sometimes used birth control during times when they did indeed want to get pregnant. Their narratives showed that lots of factors shape how people use birth control other than pregnancy desires. Indeed, there is a vast transdisciplinary literature examining the reasons why women do not use birth control when they do not desire a pregnancy. There is hardly any literature, to my knowledge, that examines the reasons that women use birth control when they would like to become pregnant. The suggestion that marginalized women's non-normative behavior results from a cultural deficit (e.g., a cultural proclivity to valorize unplanned pregnancies) is an oft-used distraction that obscures how social ideologies and practices perpetuate those injustices preventing women from having pregnancies under the conditions that they desire in the first place.

As this chapter shows, women's experiences with contraception and pregnancy are complex, intersectional, and embedded within larger gendered structures that can erode reproductive autonomy on multiple dimensions. Further, ignoring women's social contexts while championing highly effective birth control as the solution to unintended pregnancy prevents understanding of the real social and structural challenges that prevent women from contracepting to begin with.[13] Almost all women who experienced a pregnancy received gendered messages about prescription birth control, or faced partners who did not want to wear condoms at some point in their relationships. The ways that they responded to these situations—either by beginning prescription contraception or not doing so—simply differed. Elucidating their experiences demonstrated the highly gendered, classed, and racialized subjectivity deployed in automatically assuming that their decisions were misguided, careless, or wrong.

Conclusion

Something Better

As the interviews came to an end, women were asked to talk about anything that they felt would make getting birth control easier for others who wanted to prevent pregnancy. Although our question focused on women's use of birth control, it was not uncommon for them to discuss men. As Imani (26 years old, Black) said, "I would fund more studies that would promote male usage of birth control. I think it's too much . . . it puts too much of the burden on women and so I think you're creating a culture where you sort of look at the woman as being at fault for pregnancy. Just like, look at scandals with stars and their baby mommas . . . [they] could not have been pregnant [if not] for your sperm." Michele (24 years old, white) had a more blunt solution: "They should give guys a shot. That's what I think." While women wanted more support from their partners in their quests to prevent pregnancy, actual "male usage" of condoms was only part of the equation. They also believed a lack of male prescription methods contributed to their turmoil. Ongoing efforts to develop so-called male birth control might seem prescient in this context, but women's experiences being channeled into using "female methods" demonstrated that gendered approaches to birth control resulted in unintended consequences.

In *Just Get on the Pill,* I show that nature does not dictate the gendered organization of birth control, despite the pervasiveness of biological determinism in explanations for gender inequality. Instead, people are socialized into using particular forms of birth control when such an arrangement is not inevitable. Many women understood starting prescription birth control (and other methods designed for their bodies) as the logical step to take before beginning sexual relationships or after transitioning into long-term relationships. They received messages supporting such an approach—prioritizing prescription birth control over condoms for women—from mothers, partners, medical providers, and friends. Though several women aspired to use prescription methods alongside condoms, they sometimes encountered difficulty in getting partners to support their efforts because of the belief that men need not wear condoms when their partners use prescription birth control and the widespread social comfort with holding women alone accountable for preventing pregnancy. Moreover, some women had trouble using prescription birth control altogether because of dissatisfaction, discomfort with side effects, or a general disinterest in using the methods. Thus, contrary to arguments that the gender division of labor in contraception works, the women's narratives highlighted the challenges for preventing both pregnancy and disease that could result. The preceding chapters of *Just Get on the Pill* showed how social policies that divorce pregnancy prevention from sexual health and autonomy ultimately reinforce the unequal gender division of labor, perpetuate the long-standing isolation of men in public health efforts to prevent pregnancy, and fundamentally undermine campaigns to stop the spread of disease.

Highlighting the importance of intersectionality, I showed how the social acceptance of gendered compulsory birth control obscured the lived experiences of Black and low-income women as they tried to negotiate sex in the context of gender inequality. Traditional explanations for women's contraceptive motivations cannot fully account for their behaviors. An intersectional analysis grounded in reproductive justice demonstrated the logic behind their decisions. Such strategies for pregnancy prevention as expecting to use condoms rather than beginning prescription birth control in long-term relationships made sense to the women in a context in which they enacted different responses to gender inequality and were differentially affected by gendered paths of least resistance. Although these women did not always use condoms as consistently as they had hoped to do, their decisions not to begin prescription birth control made sense to them given their social location. Indeed, as Kristin Luker argued almost a half-century ago, contraceptive "risk-taking" has its origin in social factors.[1] It is a mistake to assume that these women's behaviors resulted solely from a lack of knowledge or strong motivation to prevent pregnancy.

Overlooking social structures, then, has consequences not only for social scientific understandings of gender but also for the very lives of women most affected by contemporary reproductive health policies. Beginning prescription birth control even when it means assuming primary responsibility for contraception may seem unproblematic for women who are more comfortable with the traditional gender division of labor in birth control. These women may never expect to bring and use condoms over the course of their relationships. For women who are less committed to gender expectations in birth control and have concerns about disease, however, such a tradeoff may appear much more costly. As it happens, such a tradeoff *was* more costly for the Black women in this study. Black women having unprotected intercourse were more likely to contract an STD than women of other races in the sample, which may have been a result of proximity and group-level differences in STD rates.[2] Upholding social expectations that sexually active women use prescription methods without a concomitant focus on condom use, therefore, may not serve women who neither subscribe to gendered ideologies in pregnancy prevention nor have the luxury of being carefree about disease. While reproductive rights frameworks that focus on choice fail to fully capture the complexity of women's experiences navigating sexuality and fertility, reproductive justice offers a way forward.

The power of reproductive justice is in its position as an "emergent radical theory" that "posits that intersecting forces produce differing reproductive experiences that shape each individual's life."[3] In practice, only one act affected the women's likelihood of both pregnancy and contracting a disease: intercourse without a condom. Gender socialization meant that while many women in *Just Get on the Pill* were familiar with using and accessing prescription birth control, they were much less comfortable with buying, bringing, and using condoms. Advancing women's human rights, then, necessitates supporting protections for their sexual health. This means that prevention justice *is* reproductive justice. As advocate Dazon Dixon Diallo (founder and president of Sisterlove, Inc.) has explained, prevention justice is a "framework [that] acknowledges that HIV prevention cannot be separated from human rights, thereby changing both the way we look at HIV prevention and how we advocate for it."[4] I contend that achieving reproductive justice for women of color and *all* women means that we must not make them more susceptible to disease by advancing an at-all-costs social imperative that dictates they need only prevent pregnancy. In fact, such a policy is the epitome of reproductive injustice. In the pages that follow, alongside summarizing the lessons learned, I discuss how we might remedy gendered compulsory birth control and create the kind of reproductively just society that women-of-color organizers envisioned when they began mobilizing around reproductive justice twenty-five years ago.

ENVISIONING A BETTER WAY FORWARD

Central to a reproductive justice approach is not simply documenting how injustice operates but also providing a vision for how a more just society would be organized.[5] In this section, I suggest adjustments that would help reduce gender inequality, improve health equity, and support reproductive autonomy.

The stories that I shared demonstrated the importance of transcending the individual in studies of pregnancy prevention. The sociological imagination proved key here.[6] As other feminist scholars of reproduction have argued, reproductive outcomes are not simply a consequence of the individual choices made by individual women.[7] The experiences of the women in this study highlighted the importance of thinking about pregnancy and birth prevention as *social processes* that occur in particular contexts. From this perspective, people's desire for children was only one factor that influenced behavior, and whether or not they used contraception was only one component of their experience. *Just Get on the Pill* has demonstrated that women made choices about methods based in part on larger messages about gender, and they had to weigh contraceptive properties against what use meant for their reproductive autonomy, gendered relationship to power, protection from disease, and overall sense of well-being. While they received strong messages about what they should do as women to prevent pregnancy, they received much less support in dealing with gendered violence, gendered contraceptive negotiation, or gendered constraints on their sexual freedom. In the general population, women's experiences on each of these dimensions vary based on their race, sexual orientation, socioeconomic status, and geographic location, among other social categories. For these reasons, examining birth control as a social process requires critical analyses that uncover the operation of gendered logics in research and practice, as well as attention to interlocking systems of oppression that shape people's experiences in what sociologist Patricia Hill Collins calls the matrix of domination.[8]

In my view, deconstructing "contraceptive effectiveness" as a social concept is central to uprooting hidden manifestations of gender. Contraceptive effectiveness dominates discussions about the types of birth control that women should use. The stories shared in *Just Get on the Pill*, however, demonstrated that gender inequality is fundamentally built into our very measures of contraceptive effectiveness. Though often used interchangeably, *contraceptive efficacy* relates to how well contraceptives prevent pregnancy during clinical trials, whereas *contraceptive effectiveness* relates to how well the methods work in real world settings.[9] Clinical trials measure how well the methods themselves work when people use them perfectly. For example, methods like the pill, patch, and ring are 99 percent effective when used perfectly during clinical trials (efficacy) but are only 91 percent effective in everyday practice, when people may forget to take a pill or replace a patch (effectiveness). Condoms are 98 percent effective when used perfectly ("consistently and correctly"), but 82 percent effective in practice (when people fail to do so). What focusing only on effectiveness obscures, however, is that the pill, patch, and ring are only as effective as they are in practice because *women commit to using them regularly.* As I have shown, the women in this study experienced a great deal of both pressure and support to help them do so. Likewise, IUDs and implants can only be 99 percent effective if users are willing to insert them to prevent pregnancy in the first place. Thus, recommending prescription methods only on the basis of their being more effective than condoms treats *effectiveness* as an unchangeable scientific fact, rather than as a moldable social outcome influenced in part by gender expectations of men's and women's responsibility for preventing pregnancy.

Although this gendered approach to pregnancy prevention is long-standing, public health campaigns aimed at reducing the spread of HIV suggest that there is a better way forward. Such campaigns highlight just how effective condoms are for preventing disease. Indeed, the belief that condoms are much "less effective" than prescription birth control (a belief premised on "inconsistent or incorrect use" estimates) may lead people *not* to use a form that is technically effective in protecting against both pregnancy and disease. Instead of reinforcing harmful gendered messages about prescription birth control and condoms, pregnancy prevention campaigns could stress the effectiveness of condoms when used *consistently and correctly* and encourage *all people* to use them. The Centers for Disease Control and Prevention's "Start Talking. Stop HIV." campaign provides one such example. In addition to emphasizing the importance of making a conversation about using condoms an important part of foreplay, their brochure encourages partners to talk about "safer sex, including using condoms and medicines that prevent and treat HIV."[10] It would be exceedingly easy for pregnancy prevention campaigns to do the same, emphasizing in a talk about "condoms and prescription birth control" that condoms are an effective way *to prevent pregnancy,* and not just a method that primarily provides protection against STIs. Emphasizing condom use becomes even more important given the possibility of a "male birth control pill" and research showing that advertisements for the male pill imply that users do not have to wear condoms.[11] This could help alleviate gendered compulsory birth control, increase people's protection against STDs, and provide people with support in shifting the cultural messages that link condoms to disease. Moreover, clinicians could incorporate information on contraception into young men's visits for HPV vaccines, which could both support men's health and increase shared responsibility for preventing pregnancy.

A campaign encouraging shared responsibility could also diminish the hidden institutional mechanisms that support gendered compulsory birth control for women who do not want children. As I have shown, pregnancy prevention is largely organized into methods for men and methods for women. While the Affordable Care Act requires private insurers to cover prescription contraception and tubal ligation for women without a co-pay, vasectomy is not a covered procedure. In situations in which people do not want to have more children, they may still opt for a tubal ligation rather than a vasectomy because sterilization for women is covered. This makes less sense from both a health and an economic perspective because vasectomy is less invasive and less expensive than tubal ligation.[12] Once again, women's unequal use of "female contraception" is not a consequence of "natural" differences between men's and women's bodies or of inevitable experiences of gender. While some men may opt out of vasectomy because of gendered emphases on male virility, others see it as a way to take responsibility in relationships.[13] It is important not to assume, therefore, that men will automatically be unwilling partners in contraception. As anthropologist Matthew Gutman argues, "It is a mistake to discount the active participation and empathy of men in contraception altogether."[14] Nelly Oudshoorn in fact contends in her groundbreaking book on the "male [contraceptive] pill" that we must recognize that masculinity is "multiple, complex, and fluid."[15] To support pregnancy prevention efforts by men and to reduce gender inequality in relationships, reproductive health policies must change to better account for pregnancy prevention as a process involving both partners. Providing insurance coverage for vasectomy is one way to do this.

In addition to expanding insurance coverage for both forms of sterilization, reducing gender inequality also requires providing greater resources for condom provision to people during contraceptive counseling visits. While women in the study mentioned receiving condoms during the contraceptive counseling visits in which they received prescription birth control, the number of sex acts covered by prescription birth control far exceeds the number covered by the condoms provided. Women received prescription birth control for as little as one month to as much as one year, but they usually received only "a bag of condoms." In general, condoms are also de-emphasized in contraceptive counseling visits with women.[16] Since men have fewer interactions with medical clinics than women, they may find it harder to get condoms free of charge. From a strictly economic perspective, then, couples may decide against using condoms—even during encounters in which one or both partners might prefer to use them—simply because condoms become costly in the long term. Interestingly, while all interviews in this study were conducted *before* the ACA took effect, women very rarely mentioned sharing the cost of prescription contraception with their partners. As a consequence, cutting costs by switching to prescription contraception usually meant that only one member of the couple saved money. Increasing coverage for and provision of condoms may better support couples' efforts to use them, especially in an era when prescription birth control is covered but condom provision for an equal length of time is not.

Reproductive health clinics can also implement practical strategies to better support women as they navigate the challenges associated with prescription birth control use. While several prescription methods are associated with irregular bleeding, for example, women rarely receive hygiene products. This, in turn, can either decrease the feasibility of using the methods or force low-income women to use limited resources on additional hygiene products. Financial support for clinics to provide women with tampons and sanitary napkins would help offset this unpredictable cost. In offering advice independent of side effects, clinicians might also look for opportunities to counsel men and women on the importance of using two methods of birth control, even after women begin hormonal contraception. Research shows that 44 percent of women who start using the pill—the most popular reversible birth control method—stop using it within one year.[17] As I have shown here, however, the women encountered difficulties transitioning back to using condoms after they and their partners had stopped. Counseling people about using condoms regardless of whether partners use prescription contraceptives could help reduce gendered compulsory birth control. Indeed, given that some women choose to stop or avoid using prescription birth control for reasons entirely unrelated to its effectiveness at preventing pregnancy, encouraging condom use might actually be a more effective means of preventing pregnancy for some.[18]

Changing the way that we as a society *talk* about birth control can also go a long way toward changing the gendered dynamics around use that I have documented in this book. Simply searching the Internet for "female contraception" and "male contraception" returns innumerable results. And even when adjectives for sex are not used to modify technology, researchers still separate birth control into separate spheres. Raising awareness about the way that we talk about contraception and link it to sexed bodies in research, policy documents, and interactions with patients can help ameliorate the institutional mechanisms that reinscribe gender ideologies. Rather than referring to "male condoms" and "female condoms," we might adopt alternative language. Removing explicit references to sex and using language like "internal" and "external" when referring to condoms, for example, leaves the type of condom being referred to clear, while reducing the tendency to associate condoms with particular bodies. There is more room for a person of any gender to provide condoms—whether internal or external—in this model. Or, acknowledging that all of the initial methods of prescription birth control were designed to affect women's bodies, we might also distinguish between "male" prescription birth control and "female" prescription birth control by using the language of "first-generation" and "second-generation" methods. These suggestions are neither exhaustive nor perfect, of course. The notion that we cannot think of sex-neutral ways to describe contraception in an era in which we have developed contraceptives that are more effective than any that came before, however, is neither a rational nor justifiable explanation for continuing to perpetuate biological determinism in pregnancy prevention.

Schools can also lead the way in creating change. Though what constitutes the ideal subject matter for sexual education is the subject of heated debate, and sex ed. is much more fraught in the United States than in other countries, proper education is key for achieving just outcomes.[19] Sociologist Lorena Garcia, for example, showed that young Latinas were exposed to racialized gendered stereotypes of sexuality that mattered for their experiences with their partners.[20] Comprehensive sexual education instructors can lead discussions about how gendered processes might unfold in relationships to help partners recognize in what ways they may be contributing to unequal outcomes. Research shows that the programs that do this very thing have better outcomes, both in terms of preventing pregnancy and reducing STIs, compared with programs that do not teach about gender and power.[21] In discussing condoms, instructors would do well to highlight the signs of contraceptive coercion. Women's experiences with partners who "slipped condoms off" and a lack of recognition that doing so constitutes sexual assault suggest women would benefit were lessons on contraception to include discussions about affirmative consent ("yes means yes"). Teaching young people to have explicit conversations about contraception and teaching all genders about all methods would better support young people's efforts to have healthy and fulfilling sexual experiences.

Families play an integral role in gender socialization around sexuality and, as such, can contribute to dramatic changes in the gendered organization of pregnancy prevention. Parents can teach children, regardless of their gender, about the variety of birth control methods available and can facilitate condom provision regardless of whether they encourage the use of prescription birth control methods. Parents can also be informed of the unintended consequences of disease, which may result from channeling children into different methods by gender. Their children can in fact still contract an STI even as they successfully prevent pregnancy if their partner is infected and they forego condom use. Thus, parents have a role to play in ensuring healthy, gender-equitable outcomes for their children, regardless of their children's gender identity. Like teachers, parents can also talk with children about how to recognize the signs of coercion in sexual relationships to help them avoid gendered compulsory birth control and ensure that each partner has the freedom to use condoms when desired.

For researchers, health practitioners, policy makers, and feminists of all stripes, this book serves as a call to center reproductive justice in our analyses and policy prescriptions. When talking about this project, I often received questions or challenges for pointing out that prescription birth control—a method long hailed as a central tool for the reproductive liberation of women—could actually be disempowering. This is less surprising for scholars who do work on the reproductive experiences of marginalized women, whose fertility decisions and very right to bear children have been challenged for centuries. A key takeaway from studies using a reproductive justice framework is that the question of reproductive liberation and autonomy is not always a simple question about whether particular birth control methods are empowering for women. Instead, the question to ask is under what *conditions* contraception is empowering for each partner. As feminist science and technology studies scholar Chikako Takeshita argues, contraceptives are "politically versatile" technologies.[22] As such, they are "adaptable to both feminist and non-feminist reproductive politics."[23] In uncritically arguing that prescription birth control is empowering for women simply because it interacts with their bodies and can be used covertly, feminists have sometimes been just as guilty of making essentialist assumptions about sex and gender. Reproductive justice requires recognizing that contraceptive technologies cannot fully support health and autonomy without a concomitant focus on the intersecting structures that enable and constrain behavior.[24] As I have shown, uncovering biological determinism in pregnancy prevention allows us to interrogate the harmful gendered ideologies that lead to health inequity and decrease women's control over their bodies. Doing so upholds the reproductive autonomy of all women, most especially those pathologized because they reject "female" prescription birth control altogether.

After writing a book on the harms of a gendered approach to birth control, I believe it is only fair to share a vision that models a better way forward. This is what reproductive justice praxis calls for. I offer the following thoughts in this spirit.

A reproductively just approach to birth control requires that we recognize that pregnancy prevention is a social process. It requires that we interrogate contraceptive effectiveness as a social—rather than neutral—concept. It requires that we listen to Black women. It requires that we interrogate biological explanations of inequality in every domain. It requires that we treat men as willing and necessary participants in the prevention of pregnancy and disease. It requires that we vigorously reject "His condom and Her birth control" and support contraceptive access for all. It requires that we recognize that social location affects whether contraceptives are a tool for liberation or oppression. It requires that we protect the right to abortion—and the right to parent—for all women, transmen, and gender nonconforming people for whom pregnancy is at issue. It requires that we lift up the voices and insights of reproductive justice advocates and organizations. And lastly it requires that we recognize that the hallmark of reproductive justice is the unwavering centering of reproductive freedom as an international human right. In sum, we must eradicate the pernicious tendrils of gender oppression in our relationships, schools, families, health care policies, and communities. The health and freedom of all people in our society depend on it.

Acknowledgments

I have been fascinated by the social experience of birth control since college, and this book has been, in many ways, a long time coming. I have numerous people to thank. First and foremost, I would like to thank the women whose narratives I draw on in this book for their generosity of spirit and time in sharing their stories with the research team for our study. I thank the members of the research team for their incredibly hard work seeing the study to completion. The study was supported in part by the Elfenwork Foundation's Collaboration on Poverty Research, a joint venture between the Stanford Center on Poverty and Inequality and the Multidisciplinary Program in Inequality and Social Policy at Harvard University's John F. Kennedy School of Government. I extend my gratitude for this support. Lastly, I thank the inimitable Paula England for her mentorship in conducting mixed-methods research and her generosity with the data that resulted from the project.

I thank my colleagues and former professors at Occidental College— where I completed my undergraduate work and spent the first six years of my faculty career—for their exceptional introduction to the wonders of sociology. I am particularly grateful to Lance Hannon and Dolores Trevizo, who encouraged me to pursue graduate school. This book would not have been possible without their support during the formative years of my undergraduate training. I am also grateful to Lisa Wade, whose Power and Sexuality class during my senior year at Oxy made me realize that birth control was a topic that I could study sociologically.

I have been exceedingly fortunate to count a number of incredible thinkers and people among my graduate school mentors. Paula England and Michael

Rosenfeld have offered their unwavering support and comradeship throughout my journey—challenging my thinking, pushing me to refine my arguments, and helping me ride the ups and downs of life in the academy along the way. I thank them for their support and for many conversations about the book over the years. I am also grateful to Tomás Jimenez and Corey Fields, who inspired me to think big and offered encouragement throughout the book publishing process. And, lastly, I thank Matt Snipp for ushering me through the early years of graduate school and for always supporting the angles at which I pursued my work.

The book manuscript itself benefited from the generosity of several colleagues and reviewers. I am grateful to Rene Almeling for sharing very helpful advice about the book-writing process when I was first putting the book together. Paula England, Katrina Kimport, and Jennifer Reich read an early draft of the Introduction, and their comments proved very helpful during revision. Katrina Kimport and Laury Oaks also provided exceptionally insightful feedback on the full draft of the manuscript, which helped me refine my arguments and added analytical depth. I also thank Jennifer Eggerling-Boeck at Harvest Editing whose comments on the penultimate draft of the Introduction helped me surface still-implicit components of my argument. I am very grateful to my writing group—Scholars Network for Reproductive Justice—which includes Anu Manchikanti Gomez, Zakiya Luna, and LaKisha Simmons. They read drafts of nearly every chapter in the book as I wrote them, and their insight, companionship, and expertise were central to the book's development. I also thank Rickie Solinger, Ruby Tapia, Khiara M. Bridges, Naomi Schneider, and the reviewers at the University of California Press for their support of the project. I also thank Ann Donahue for providing superb copy edits.

Opportunities to present ideas from the book at various venues over the years were very helpful in shaping the framing of the project. A plenary session at the 2016 Sociologists for Women in Society winter meeting, under the presidency of Adia Harvey Wingfield, offered the first opportunity to articulate an early version of the critique of social approaches to pregnancy prevention that I present in this book. A presentation at Advancing New Standards in Reproductive Health during the summer of 2015 gave me an opportunity to present some of the data from chapter 4, and the community of scholars were incredibly warm and welcoming. I'm particularly grateful to Carole Joffe and Katrina

Kimport for expressing enthusiasm about the book project when I was still in the early stages of articulating my ideas. I extend this gratitude, too, to Eviatar Zeruvabel and Joanna Kempner, whose warmth and encouragement when I presented the first draft of the manuscript in 2017 motivated me to keep moving on revisions. I also benefited from inspiring and insightful conversations about the book during a colloquium visit to the University of Delaware in 2018. An American Association of University Women American Research Publication Grant proved instrumental in getting the draft finished. I am exceedingly grateful for the generosity of the funders.

While writing the book, I was fortunate to have many colleagues who offered moral support, encouragement, and empathy during the overwhelming periods that often accompany a project of this magnitude. My colleagues at Occidental—John Lang, John Liu, Richard Mora, and Kristi Upson-Saia—were ever enthusiastic about my work and offered valuable comments. Jane Hong, Ross Lerner, and Kelema Moses offered support and helped me sustain momentum during the busy teaching term. My coworking colleagues and the staff at Cross Campus, where I spent many months painstakingly writing the book over countless lattes, were exceedingly generous in sharing their curiosity about my research. Their interest in the book and assertions that it would be important to people beyond the academy inspired me to ensure that I maintained my commitment to the book's accessibility and made theoretical concepts understandable for nonacademic readers. At the University of Oregon, I thank C.J. Pascoe, Jessica Vasquez-Tokos, and Richard York for enriching conversations about publishing and the arguments that I make in the book.

I also thank many wonderful friends for the contributions that they made to getting this book to the finish line. Lorena Castro, Eric Grollman, Rebecca Hetey, Sharon Jank, Ariela Schachter, Leanne Watt, and Rachel Wright provided warmth and encouragement throughout the process and did not balk at the prospect of my writing an original book that was not based on my dissertation and that involved analyzing so much data. Weekly accountability meetings with Eric in the thick of writing the book were tremendous. Everyone's assurances that I was doing important work and that it would one day come together were vital in maintaining the momentum required to work on a single project for nearly a decade. I thank Shavonda Joyner and Rachel

Johnson-Farias for their belief in Black girl magic, their long-standing friendship, and their insights into the processes that I describe in the book. I also thank my student Benjamin Weiss for consistently reminding me to be awe inspired by the processes unfolding in the social world and for the privilege to be among those who document and interrogate them.

Lastly, I extend my gratitude most of all to my family. My parents—Letha Hamer and Roland Littlejohn—instilled a deep appreciation for intellectual pursuits and demonstrated the importance of challenging classist understandings of intellectualism. My grandmother—Shirlese Hamer—demonstrated an unwavering commitment to education and fought to ensure that her grandchildren took advantage of educational opportunities of which she was deprived simply because she was born Black in a different time. I thank my sisters, Brandi Gutierrez and Siobhan Littlejohn, for supporting my "disappearances" whenever I get deep in thought. I thank Brandi, especially, for teaching me about reproductive justice before we even had the words to articulate its meaning. I thank Siobhan for our countless conversations about the book, her patience with me as I struggled to talk through half-baked ideas whenever she would listen, and for reading every draft of everything I ever wrote for this book. She, more than anyone, has seen this book through from beginning to end. I owe her a great debt. And lastly, I thank Francisco. His stalwart support has fundamentally shaped my freedom to think, the trajectory of my career, and the completion of this book. I thank him for being an exceptional life partner and for tolerating me with humor during my countless "in-the-zone" moments over the years, when I was oblivious to anything other than solving the puzzle that occupied my mind at the time. It takes a great deal of self-confidence and selflessness to do so with grace, love, and compassion. My thanks to all of you for believing that this girl from the projects could do whatever she wanted to—including becoming an academic and writing a book.

APPENDIX

Data and Methods

The arguments about gender and pregnancy prevention that I make in this book are based on interviews with young women conducted by a larger research team between 2009 and 2011. The team was affiliated with Stanford University and the University of California, Berkeley. I was the graduate student project manager of the research team. Paula England was the principal investigator. Other members of the team included Joanna Reed, Brooke Conroy Bass, Maja Falcon, Kate Weisshaar, Atticus Lee, Amelia Herrera, Stevie Wasson, Shanayna Harnage, and Alexandra Santa Ana.

The goal of the larger study was to understand women's experiences contracepting when they did not desire a pregnancy. To this end, the interview guide asked detailed retrospective questions about women's use of contraception with each sexual partner, history of pregnancy, experiences with side effects, and other issues bearing on reproduction. Interviewers also asked women about their attitudes toward cohabitation and marriage, as well as their plans for the future. As findings from the larger study were intended to provide insight into the factors influencing inconsistent contraceptive use, the study was limited to young, unmarried women who had experienced sexual intercourse with a man or who had experienced a pregnancy. In order to include participants across a range of socioeconomic backgrounds, participants were recruited from two community colleges and two four-year universities, as the former typically serve a broader swath of working-class and low-income women. My own interest in the data was to examine women's embodied experiences of contraception and their perceptions of satisfaction with highly effective methods like the pill.

In total, the research team interviewed 103 women, spread roughly evenly across the four sites: 15 women were Asian, 25 were Black, 18 were Latina, 2 were Native American, and 43 were white. They came from a range of socioeconomic backgrounds, with 32 from poor and working-class backgrounds and the remainder from middle-class and upper-middle-class backgrounds. By design, roughly half of the women had experienced a pregnancy and half had not. All women in the sample had used a form of contraception at some point in their lives; similar to estimates from nationally representative surveys, the vast majority of women (85%) had used a highly effective method. Interviews ranged from one to three hours long and were usually conducted on campus or at a comfortable location chosen by participants. A professional transcription company transcribed all interviews verbatim shortly after the interviews were conducted. This resulted in 3,674 pages of interview data. I quote 55 women in the manuscript but drew on all of the transcripts in the analysis.

Sex and gender emerged as explanatory frames in the course of analyses that spanned several years. Over a three-year period, I read each of the transcripts multiple times, taking note of the kinds of insights that I gained with each new reading (via analytic memoing). My constructionist approach, which treats meaning as fluid and interactional, was particularly well-suited to uncovering the hidden meaning of bodies and body parts in women's experiences of contraception. Using a combination of modified grounded theory and abductive analytic techniques, I allowed early themes to emerge from the data and read extensively in the field thereafter to aid in the generation of theory.[1] While the significance of gender was immediately apparent during the first round of analysis, the importance of bodies emerged only in later readings. Highlighting processes typically taken for granted, of course, is one of the strengths of abductive analyses.[2]

To establish a backdrop for the relationship between contraception, bodies, and gender, I also relied on historical materials. I read articles from as early as the 1920s from medical journals like the *American Journal of Obstetrics and Gynecology,* and also researched official policy positions on contraception from organizations like the American Academy of Pediatrics. I also did a targeted review of other historical materials, including medical textbooks, which I identified via secondary research on the history of contraception. Lastly, I gained insight into the evolution of contraception as a medical, rather than lay, priority during the late nineteenth and early twentieth centuries by reviewing historical documents from the digital archives of the American Medical Association.

Notes

Introduction

1. Martinez and Abma, "Sexual Activity."
2. Kusunoki and Barber, "Dynamics of Intimate Relationships."
3. Higgins and Smith, "Sexual Acceptability of Contraception."
4. Fennell, "Men Bring Condoms"; Reed et al., "Consistent and Inconsistent Contraception."
5. Higgins and Cooper, "Dual Use of Condoms"; Mosher, Jones, and Abma, "Intended and Unintended Births."
6. Bertotti, "Gendered Divisions."
7. Solinger, *Pregnancy and Power.*
8. American Medical Association, "House of Delegates Proceedings."
9. Santelli et al., "Measurement and Meaning."
10. Tone, *Devices and Desires.*
11. Hartmann, *Reproductive Rights and Wrongs*; Roberts, *Killing the Black Body*; Schoen, *Choice and Coercion.*
12. Stern, "Planning the Unplanned Pregnancy."
13. Brown and Eisenberg, *Best Intentions.*
14. Brown and Eisenberg, *Best Intentions,* 3.
15. Brown and Eisenberg, *Best Intentions,* 3.
16. Finer and Zolna, "Declines in Unintended Pregnancy."
17. Finer and Zolna, "Declines in Unintended Pregnancy."
18. Finer and Zolna, "Declines in Unintended Pregnancy."
19. Sonfield, Hasstedt, and Benson Gold, *Moving Forward.*

20. Sedgh, Singh, and Hussain, "Intended and Unintended Pregnancies"; Trussell, "Cost of Unintended Pregnancy."

21. Solinger, *Wake Up Little Susie;* and *Pregnancy and Power.*

22. Logan et al., *Consequences of Unintended Childbearing.*

23. US Department of Health and Human Services, *Healthy People 2020.*

24. Miller, "Ten Goals," 3.

25. Miller, "Ten Goals," 3.

26. Gavin et al., "Providing Quality Family Planning."

27. American Academy of Pediatrics, "Contraception for Adolescents"; Centers for Disease Control and Prevention, "Sexually Transmitted Disease Surveillance 2014."

28. Trussell et al., "Burden of Unintended Pregnancy."

29. Waggoner, *Zero Trimester.*

30. Guttmacher Institute, "Facts."

31. Guttmacher Institute, "Facts."

32. Reeves and Krause, "What's Stopping American Men?" "Highly effective methods" include hormonal contraceptives and IUDs, which virtually eliminate the likelihood of pregnancy when used as intended.

33. Mills, *Sociological Imagination,* 159.

34. Rubin, "Traffic in Women," 159.

35. Ross, "Understanding Reproductive Justice," 14.

36. Asian Communities for Reproductive Justice, "New Vision," 5.

37. Ross et al., *Radical Reproductive Justice.*

38. Ross, "Understanding Reproductive Justice."

39. Luna, "From Rights to Justice"; Price, "What Is Reproductive Justice?"; Ross and Solinger, *Reproductive Justice;* Smith, "Beyond Pro-choice."

40. Colen, "'With Respect and Feelings'"; Ginsburg and Rapp, *Conceiving the New World Order;* Twine, *Outsourcing the Womb.*

41. Luna and Luker, "Reproductive Justice," 342.

42. Ross and Solinger, *Reproductive Justice,* 69–70.

43. United Nations, "Report," 36.

44. Asian Communities for Reproductive Justice, "New Vision," 3.

45. Ross and Solinger, *Reproductive Justice.*

46. Barcelos and Gubrium, "Reproducing Stories"; Bridges, "Quasi Colonial Bodies"; Bridges, *Reproducing Race.*

47. Luna and Luker, "Reproductive Justice"; Ross et al., "'SisterSong Collective'"; Ross and Solinger, *Reproductive Justice.*

48. I am sensitive to my position as a gatekeeper in that I have the power both to contribute to knowledge and to help determine what constitutes knowledge itself as a researcher. Thus, a Black feminist epistemology, as I deploy it in *Just Get on the Pill,* refers to valuing and seamlessly integrating multiple forms of knowledge, especially the experiential knowledge possessed by marginalized women. It means assuming I could potentially learn just as much about the social world from listening to women as I could from reading research studies about their lives. To illustrate, readers will note that I often integrate women's narratives with my discussion of research studies, rather than setting the data apart as evidence and giving the impression that "true knowledge" is created by researchers. Lastly, adopting a Black feminist epistemology means that I did not assume I knew about the motivations undergirding women's contraceptive decisions simply because I knew a lot about the research studying said motivations. This proved particularly useful for the analysis in chapter 4, where an overreliance on what scholars call "expert knowledge" would have led me to overlook the experiential knowledge that guided the behavior of women, who are often written off as "bad" or "irresponsible" users of contraception.

Chapter 1: His Condom

1. Garcia, *Respect Yourself, Protect Yourself;* Marston and King, "Factors"; Woodsong and Koo, "Two Good Reasons."

2. Twenge, Sherman, and Wells, "Changes." See Littlejohn, "'It's Those Pills'"; and Tavory and Swidler, "Condom Semiotics" for exceptions.

3. Reece et al., "Condom Use Rates."

4. Carter, "Gender Socialization"; Lorber, *Paradoxes of Gender;* Mora, "'Do It for All!'"

5. Hamilton and Armstrong, "Gendered Sexuality"; Nack, *Damaged Goods.*

6. Kreager and Staff, "Sexual Double Standard."

7. Erdmans and Black, *On Becoming.*

8. Hlavka, "Normalizing Sexual Violence."

9. Centers for Disease Control and Prevention, "Contraception."

10. Centers for Disease Control and Prevention, "Contraception."

11. American Academy of Pediatrics, "Contraception for Adolescents."

12. American College of Obstetricians and Gynecologists, "Increasing Access."

13. For research about men's use of "female" condoms, see Gibson et al., "Experiences of 100 Men"; and Wolitski et al., "Awareness and Use." For men's preference for the female condom, see Gibson et al., "Experiences of 100 Men"; and Renzi et al., "Safety and Acceptability." Note that while neither the female nor male condom is approved for anal sex, this point is immaterial to the point that the condom need not refer to male or female bodies.

14. Oudshoorn, Rommes, and Stienstra, "Configuring the User."

15. Lowe, "Contraception and Heterosex." This is part and parcel of practicing normative heterosexuality as heteronormativity, which operates broadly through regulating gender (Butler, *Undoing Gender*).

16. "XOXO by Trojan," Trojan Brand Condoms, accessed December 14, 2020, https://www.trojanbrands.com/en-ca/condoms/xoxo-by-trojan-condoms.

17. Schonbrun, "XOXO Campaign," n.p.

18. Carpenter, *Virginity Lost*; Mollborn, *Mixed Messages*.

19. DeNora, *Making Sense of Reality*; Friedman, *Blind to Sameness*; Rubin, "Traffic in Women."

20. PATH, UNFPA, "Female Condom."

21. See, for example, Mollborn, *Mixed Messages*.

22. The 40 percent statistic does not include instances of women treating men's condom use as something that "he did," if they were simply responding to the less frequent instances in which it was the interviewer who framed the question in that way (e.g., "Did *he* use a condom?").

23. Higgins and Hirsch, "Pleasure, Power, and Inequality."

24. PerryUndem, *Contraceptives and Policy*.

25. K. Davis et al., "Qualitative Examination."

26. As discussed in Lowe, "Contraception and Heterosex."

27. Fitch et al., "Condom Effectiveness."

28. Centers for Disease Control and Prevention, *Sexually Transmitted Disease Surveillance, 2015*.

29. Nack, *Damaged Goods*.

Chapter 2: Her Birth Control

1. Collins, "Black Feminist Epistemology"; Duran, *Toward a Feminist Epistemology.*
2. Boonstra et al., "Abortion in Women's Lives."
3. Kimport, Weitz, and Freeman, "Stratified Legitimacy of Abortions."
4. S. Jackson, "Gender, Sexuality and Heterosexuality."
5. Luker, *Taking Chances*, 124.
6. Luker, *Taking Chances.*
7. Shtulman, *Scienceblind.*
8. Pazol, Kramer, and Hogue, "Condoms for Dual Protection."
9. Mann and Grzanka, "Agency-without-Choice."
10. Littlejohn, "Hormonal Contraceptive Use."
11. Lessard et al., "Contraceptive Features."
12. Jackson et al., "Racial and Ethnic Differences."
13. Beksinska et al., "Prospective Study"; Berenson and Rahman, "Changes in Weight"; Gallo et al., "Combination Contraceptives."
14. Grimes and Schulz, "Nonspecific Side Effects."
15. Littlejohn, "'It's Those Pills.'"
16. Hochschild, *Managed Heart.*
17. Kimport, "Male Body-Based Contraceptives."
18. Kimport, "More than a Physical Burden."

Chapter 3: Don't Be a Bitch

1. Dickinson, "Contraception," 589.
2. Dickinson added that "for the careless and the poor it may be of little reliance but as a preventive of venereal disease [it] has no competitor" (589).
3. Masters et al., "Correlates."
4. Laslett and Brenner, "Gender and Social Reproduction."
5. Sewell, "Theory of Structure."
6. Defining responsibility for preventing pregnancy and birth is a complex issue. In the public health era, one might argue that multiple actors believe they have a responsibility for preventing "unintended" conceptions, from

government agencies and clinicians to teachers and parents. I focus on responsibility at the dyadic level: who takes action in the relationship to contracept and who bears the costs of contracepting? Thus, parents who drive women to appointments play a crucial role in *facilitating* prescription birth control use for women. In my assessment of current social expectations, however, women themselves ultimately bear responsibility for preventing pregnancy and face the blame when they fail to do so.

7. G. Davis, *Contesting Intersex.*

8. Peipert et al., "Continuation and Satisfaction."

9. Oudshoorn discusses this in *The Male Pill.*

10. On gendered norms, see Mollborn, *Mixed Messages*; on normatively gendered sexuality, see Kimport, Weitz, and Freeman, "Stratified Legitimacy of Abortions."

11. Orenstein, *Girls & Sex.*

12. Brodsky, "'Rape-Adjacent.'"

13. Reed et al., "Consistent and Inconsistent Contraception," and Sobo, *Choosing Unsafe Sex,* both discuss the social expectations around condom use in long-term relationships.

14. Silliman, "Policing the National Body"; Silliman et al., *Undivided Rights.*

15. Denbow, *Governed through Choice,* 11.

16. Reagan, *When Abortion Was a Crime.*

17. Gramsci and Hobsbawm, *Gramsci Reader.*

Chapter 4: Selective Selection

Epigraph: Roberts, *Killing the Black Body,* 8.

1. D.-A. Davis, *Reproductive Injustice.*

2. Link and Phelan, "Social Conditions."

3. West and Zimmerman, "Doing Gender."

4. Nakano Glenn, "Social Construction and Institutionalization," 9.

5. Butler, *Undoing Gender;* Deutsch, "Undoing Gender."

6. Franklin, "African Americans."

7. Frye, "Missing Conversation about Work."

8. Daniels, Mosher, and Jones, *Contraceptive Methods.*

9. Frost, Singh, and Finer, "Factors."

10. Mosher et al., "Use of Contraception."

11. Higgins, "Pregnancy Ambivalence"; Higgins and Smith, "Sexual Acceptability of Contraception."

12. Manlove et al., "Relationship Characteristics."

13. American College of Obstetricians and Gynecologists, "Contraceptive Counseling."

Conclusion

1. Luker, *Taking Chances*, 112.

2. Hogben and Leichliter, "Social Determinants"; Centers for Disease Control and Prevention, *Sexually Transmitted Disease Surveillance, 2015*.

3. Ross et al., *Radical Reproductive Justice*, 13, 15.

4. Diallo, "HIV Prevention," 342.

5. Ross et al., *Radical Reproductive Justice*.

6. Mills, *Sociological Imagination*.

7. Denbow, *Governed through Choice*; Oaks, *Giving Up Baby*.

8. Collins, *Black Feminist Thought*.

9. Hatcher et al., *Contraceptive Technology*.

10. Centers for Disease Control and Prevention, "Start Talking. Stop HIV."

11. Oaks, "Manhood and Meaning"; Oudshoorn, "Imagined Men."

12. Reeves and Krause, "What's Stopping American Men?"

13. Terry and Braun, "'Taking Responsibility.'"

14. Gutmann, *Fixing Men*, 39.

15. Oudshoorn, *Male Pill*, 239.

16. Kimport, "Talking."

17. Peipert et al., "Continuation and Satisfaction."

18. Manchikanti Gomez, Mann, and Torres, "'It Would Have Control.'"

19. For discussions of sexual education content, see Doan and Williams, *Politics of Virginity*; Fields, *Risky Lessons*; and Irvine, *Talk about Sex*. For how sexual education in the United States differs from that in other countries, see Luker, *When Sex Goes to School*.

20. Garcia, *Respect Yourself*, 17.

21. Haberland, "Case for Addressing Gender."

22. Takeshita, *Global Biopolitics*.

23. Takeshita, *Global Biopolitics*, 3.

24. Nelson, *More than Medicine.*

Appendix

1. Charmaz, *Constructing Grounded Theory;* Timmermans and Tavory, "Theory Construction in Qualitative Research."

2. Timmermans and Tavory, "Theory Construction in Qualitative Research."

Bibliography

American Academy of Pediatrics. "Contraception for Adolescents." *Pediatrics* 134 (2014): e1244–56.

American College of Obstetricians and Gynecologists. "Contraceptive Counseling: Position Statement." Washington, DC, 2016.

———. "Increasing Access to Contraceptive Implants and Intrauterine Devices to Reduce Unintended Pregnancy: Committee Opinion No. 642." *Obstetrics and Gynecology* 126 (2015): e44–48.

American Medical Association. *House of Delegates Proceedings, Annual Meeting*. 1937. Digital Archives. American Medical Association. https://ama.nmtvault.com/jsp/PsBrowse.jsp.

Asian Communities for Reproductive Justice. "A New Vision for Advancing Our Movement for Reproductive Health, Reproductive Rights, and Reproductive Justice." Oakland, CA: ACRJ, 2005. https://forwardtogether.org/wp-content/uploads/2017/12/ACRJ-A-New-Vision.pdf.

Barcelos, Chris A., and Aline C. Gubrium. "Reproducing Stories: Strategic Narratives of Teen Pregnancy and Motherhood." *Social Problems* 61, no. 3 (2014): 466–81.

Beksinska, Mags E., Jenni A. Smit, Immo Kleinschmidt, Cecilia Milford, and Timothy M. M. Farley. "Prospective Study of Weight Change in New Adolescent Users of DMPA, NET-EN, COCs, Nonusers and Discontinuers of Hormonal Contraception." *Contraception* 81, no. 1 (2010): 30–34. https://doi.org/10.1016/j.contraception.2009.07.007.

Berenson, Abbey B., and Mahbubur Rahman. "Changes in Weight, Total Fat, Percent Body Fat, and Central-to-Peripheral Fat Ratio Associated with

Injectable and Oral Contraceptive Use." *American Journal of Obstetrics and Gynecology* 200, no. 3 (2009): 329.e1–e8.

Bertotti, Andrea M. "Gendered Divisions of Fertility Work: Socioeconomic Predictors of Female versus Male Sterilization." *Journal of Marriage and Family* 75, no. 1 (February 6, 2013): 13–25.

Boonstra, Heather D., Rachel Benson Gold, Cory L. Richards, and Lawrence B. Finer. *Abortion in Women's Lives*. New York: Guttmacher Institute, 2006.

Bridges, Khiara M. "Quasi Colonial Bodies: An Analysis of the Reproductive Lives of Poor Black and Racially Subjugated Women." *Columbia Journal of Gender and Law* 18, no. 2 (2009): 609–46.

———. *Reproducing Race: An Ethnography of Pregnancy as a Site of Racialization*. Berkeley: University of California Press, 2011.

Brodsky, Alexandra. "'Rape-Adjacent': Imagining Legal Responses to Nonconsensual Condom Removal." *Columbia Journal of Gender and Law* 32, no. 2 (2017): 183–210.

Brown, Sarah S., and Leon Eisenberg, eds. *The Best Intentions: Unintended Pregnancy and the Well-Being of Children and Families*. Washington, DC: National Academy Press, 1995.

Butler, Judith. *Undoing Gender*. New York: Routledge, 2004.

Carpenter, Laura. *Virginity Lost: An Intimate Portrait of First Sexual Experiences*. New York: New York University Press, 2005.

Carter, Michael. "Gender Socialization and Identity Theory." *Social Sciences* 3 (2014): 242–63.

Centers for Disease Control and Prevention. "Contraception." Website for the Centers for Disease Control and Prevention. Last reviewed August 13, 2020. https://www.cdc.gov/reproductivehealth/contraception/.

———. *Sexually Transmitted Disease Surveillance, 2013*. Atlanta: US Department of Health and Human Services, 2014. https://www.cdc.gov/std /stats/archive/Surv2013-Print.pdf.

———. *Sexually Transmitted Disease Surveillance, 2014*. Atlanta: US Department of Health and Human Services, 2015. https://www.cdc.gov/std/stats /archive/surv-2014-print.PDF.

———. *Sexually Transmitted Disease Surveillance, 2015*. Atlanta: US Department of Health and Human Services, 2016. https://www.cdc.gov/std /stats/archive/STD-Surveillance-2015-print.pdf.

———. "Start Talking. Stop HIV: A Campaign Encouraging Gay and Bisexual Men to Talk Openly about HIV." Atlanta: US Department of Health and Human Services, n.d. https://www.cdc.gov/stophivtogether/library/start-talking-stop-hiv/brochures/cdc-lsht-stsh-brochure-campaign.pdf.

Charmaz, Kathy. *Constructing Grounded Theory*. 2nd ed. Thousand Oaks, CA: Sage, 2014.

Colen, Shellee. "'With Respect and Feelings': Voices of West Indian Child Care and Domestic Workers in New York City." In *All American Women: Lines That Divide, Ties That Bind,* edited by Johnnetta B. Cole, 46–70. New York: Free Press, 1986.

Collins, Patricia Hill. "Black Feminist Epistemology." In *Contemporary Sociological Theory,* edited by Joseph Gerteis, Craig Calhoun, James Moody, Steven Pfaff, and Indermohan Virk, 327–36. 2nd ed. Malden, MA: Blackwell, 2007.

———. *Black Feminist Thought: Knowledge, Consciousness, and the Politics of Empowerment.* New York: Routledge, 2002.

Daniels, Kimberly, William D. Mosher, and Jo Jones. *Contraceptive Methods Women Have Ever Used: United States, 1982–2010.* National Health Statistics Reports, no. 62. Atlanta: US Department of Health and Human Services, Centers for Disease Control and Prevention, National Center for Health Statistics, 2013.

Davis, Dána-Ain. *Reproductive Injustice: Racism, Pregnancy, and Premature Birth.* New York: New York University Press, 2019.

Davis, Georgiann. *Contesting Intersex: The Dubious Diagnosis.* New York: New York University Press, 2015.

Davis, Kelly Cue, Trevor J. Schraufnagel, Kelly F. Kajumulo, Amanda K. Gilmore, Jeanette Norris, and William H. George. "A Qualitative Examination of Men's Condom Use Attitudes and Resistance: 'It's Just Part of the Game.'" *Archives of Sexual Behavior* 43, no. 3 (2014): 631–43.

Denbow, Jennifer M. *Governed through Choice: Autonomy, Technology, and the Politics of Reproduction.* New York: New York University Press, 2015.

DeNora, Tia. *Making Sense of Reality: Culture and Perception in Everyday Life.* Thousand Oaks, CA: Sage, 2014.

Deutsch, Francine M. "Undoing Gender." *Gender and Society* 21, no. 1 (2007): 106–27.

Diallo, Dixon Dazon. "HIV Prevention and Reproductive Justice: A Framework for Saving Women's Lives." In *Radical Reproductive Justice: Foundation, Theory, Practice, Critique,* edited by Loretta Ross, Erika Derkas, Whitney Peoples, Lynn Roberts, and Pamela Bridgewater, 340–46. New York: Feminist Press, 2017.

Dickinson, Robert. "Contraception: A Medical Review of the Situation." *American Journal of Obstetrics and Gynecology* 8, no. 5 (1924): 583–604.

Doan, Alesha E., and Jean Calterone Williams. *The Politics of Virginity: Abstinence in Sex Education.* Westport, CT: Praeger, 2008.

Duran, Jane. *Toward a Feminist Epistemology.* Lanham, MD: Rowman and Littlefield, 1991.

Erdmans, Mary Patrice, and Timothy Black. *On Becoming a Teen Mom: Life before Pregnancy.* Berkeley: University of California Press, 2015.

Fennell, Julie Lynn. "Men Bring Condoms, Women Take Pills: Men's and Women's Roles in Contraceptive Decision Making." *Gender and Society* 25, no. 4 (August 1, 2011): 496–521. https://doi.org/10.1177/0891243211416113.

Fields, Jessica. *Risky Lessons: Sex Education and Social Inequality.* New Brunswick, NJ: Rutgers University Press, 2008.

Finer, Lawrence B., and Mia R. Zolna. "Declines in Unintended Pregnancy in the United States, 2008–2011." *New England Journal of Medicine* 374, no. 9 (March 3, 2016): 843–52. https://doi.org/10.1056/NEJMsa1506575.

Fitch, J. Thomas, Curtis Stine, W. David Hager, Joshua Mann, Mary B. Adam, and Joe McIlhaney. "Condom Effectiveness: Factors That Influence Risk Reduction." *Sexually Transmitted Diseases* 29, no. 12 (2002): 811–17.

Franklin, Donna. "African Americans and the Birth of the Modern Marriage." In *Families as They Really Are,* edited by Barbara J. Risman and Virginia Rutter, 63–74. New York: W. W. Norton, 2015.

Friedman, Asia. *Blind to Sameness: Sexpectations and the Social Construction of Male and Female Bodies.* Chicago: University of Chicago Press, 2013.

Frost, Jennifer J., Susheela Singh, and Lawrence B. Finer. "Factors Associated with Contraceptive Use and Nonuse, United States, 2004." *Perspectives on Sexual and Reproductive Health* 39, no. 2 (2007): 90–99. https://doi.org/10.2307/30042942.

Frye, Jocelyn. "The Missing Conversation about Work and Family: Unique Challenges Facing Women of Color." Washington, DC: Center for American Progress, 2016.

Gallo, M. F., L. M. Lopez, D. A. Grimes, F. Carayon, K. F. Schulz, and F. M. Helmerhorst. "Combination Contraceptives: Effects on Weight." *Cochrane Database of Systematic Reviews*, no. 1 (2014). https://doi.org /10.1002/14651858.CD003987.pub5.

Garcia, Lorena. *Respect Yourself, Protect Yourself: Latina Girls and Sexual Identity.* New York: New York University Press, 2012.

Gavin, Loretta, Susan Moskosky, Marion Carter, Kathryn Curtis, Evelyn Glass, Emily Godfrey, and Arik Marcell, et al. "Providing Quality Family Planning Services: Recommendations of CDC and the U.S. Office of Population Affairs." *Morbidity and Mortality Weekly Report: Recommendations and Reports* 63, no. 4 (2014): 1–54.

Gibson, S., W. McFarland, D. Wohlfeiler, K. Scheer, and M. H. Katz. "Experiences of 100 Men Who Have Sex with Men Using the Reality Condom for Anal Sex." *AIDS Education and Prevention: Official Publication of the International Society for AIDS Education* 11, no. 1 (February 1999): 65–71.

Ginsburg, Faye D., and Rayna Rapp, eds. *Conceiving the New World Order: The Global Politics of Reproduction.* Berkeley: University of California Press, 1995.

Gramsci, Antonio, and Eric J. Hobsbawm. *The Antonio Gramsci Reader: Selected Writings 1916–1935.* Edited by David Forgacs. New York: New York University Press, 2000.

Grimes, David A., and Kenneth F. Schulz. "Nonspecific Side Effects of Oral Contraceptives: Nocebo or Noise?" *Contraception* 83, no. 1 (2011): 5–9.

Gutmann, Matthew C. *Fixing Men: Sex, Birth Control, and AIDS in Mexico.* Berkeley: University of California Press, 2007.

Guttmacher Institute. "Facts on Young Men's Sexual and Reproductive Health." New York: Guttmacher Institute, June 2008.

Haberland, Nicole A. "The Case for Addressing Gender and Power in Sexuality and HIV Education: A Comprehensive Review of Evaluation Studies." *International Perspectives on Sexual and Reproductive Health* 41, no. 1 (2015): 31–42.

Hamilton, Laura, and Elizabeth A. Armstrong. "Gendered Sexuality in Young Adulthood: Double Binds and Flawed Options." *Gender and Society* 23, no. 5 (2009): 589–616. https://doi.org/10.1177/0891243209345829.

Hartmann, Betsy. *Reproductive Rights and Wrongs: The Global Politics of Population Control.* Boston: South End Press, 1995.

Hatcher, Robert A., James Trussell, Anita L. Nelson, Willard Cates Jr., Felicia H. Stewart, and Deborah Kowal, eds. *Contraceptive Technology.* New York: Ardent Media, 2008.

Higgins, Jenny A. "Pregnancy Ambivalence and Long-Acting Reversible Contraceptive (LARC) Use among Young Adult Women: A Qualitative Study." *Perspectives on Sexual and Reproductive Health* 49, no. 3 (2017): 149–56. https://doi.org/10.1363/psrh.12025.

Higgins, Jenny A., and Anne D. Cooper. "Dual Use of Condoms and Contraceptives in the USA." *Sexual Health* 9, no. 1 (2012): 73–80.

Higgins, Jenny A., and Jennifer S. Hirsch. "Pleasure, Power, and Inequality: Incorporating Sexuality into Research on Contraceptive Use." *American Journal of Public Health* 98, no. 10 (2008): 1803–13.

Higgins, Jenny A., and Nicole K. Smith. "The Sexual Acceptability of Contraception: Reviewing the Literature and Building a New Concept." *Journal of Sex Research* 53, no. 4–5 (May 3, 2016): 417–56. https://doi.org/10.1080/00224499.2015.1134425.

Hlavka, Heather R. "Normalizing Sexual Violence: Young Women Account for Harassment and Abuse." *Gender and Society* 28, no. 3 (June 2014): 337–48. First published online February 28, 2014. https://doi.org/10.1177/0891243214526468.

Hochschild, Arlie Russell. *The Managed Heart: Commercialization of Human Feeling.* 3rd ed. Berkeley: University of California Press, 2012.

Hogben, Matthew, and Jami S. Leichliter. "Social Determinants and Sexually Transmitted Disease Disparities." *Sexually Transmitted Diseases* 35, no. 12 (2008): S13–S18.

Irvine, Janice M. *Talk about Sex: The Battles over Sex Education in the United States.* Oakland: University of California Press, 2002.

Jackson, Andrea V., Deborah Karasek, Christine Dehlendorf, and Diana Greene Foster. "Racial and Ethnic Differences in Women's Preferences for Features of Contraceptive Methods." *Contraception* 93, no. 5 (2016): 406–11. https://doi.org/10.1016/j.contraception.2015.12.010.

Jackson, Stevi. "Gender, Sexuality and Heterosexuality: The Complexity (and Limits) of Heteronormativity." *Feminist Theory* 7, no. 1 (2006): 105–21. https://doi.org/10.1177/1464700106061462.

Kimport, Katrina. "More than a Physical Burden: Women's Mental and Emotional Work in Preventing Pregnancy." *Journal of Sex Research* 15, no. 9 (2017): 1–10.

———. "Talking about Male Body-Based Contraceptives: The Contraceptive Counseling Visit and the Feminization of Contraception." *Social Science and Medicine* 201 (2018): 44–50.

Kimport, Katrina, Tracy A. Weitz, and Lori Freedman. "The Stratified Legitimacy of Abortions." *Journal of Health and Social Behavior* 57, no. 4 (December 1, 2016): 503–16. https://doi.org/10.1177/0022146516669970.

Kreager, Derek A., and Jeremy Staff. "The Sexual Double Standard and Adolescent Peer Acceptance." *Social Psychology Quarterly* 72, no. 2 (2009): 143–64. https://doi.org/10.1177/019027250907200205.

Kusunoki, Yasamin, and Jennifer Barber. "The Dynamics of Intimate Relationships and Contraceptive Use during Early Emerging Adulthood." *Demography* (2020). Advance Online Publication. https://doi.org/10.1007/s13524-020-00916-1.

Laslett, Barbara, and Johanna Brenner. "Gender and Social Reproduction: Historical Perspectives." *Annual Review of Sociology* 15, no. 1 (1989): 381–404.

Lessard, Lauren N., Deborah Karasek, Sandi Ma, Philip Darney, Julianna Deardorff, Maureen Lahiff, Dan Grossman, and Diana Greene Foster. "Contraceptive Features Preferred by Women at High Risk of Unintended Pregnancy." *Perspectives on Sexual and Reproductive Health* 44, no. 3 (2012): 194–200.

Link, Bruce G., and Jo Phelan. "Social Conditions as Fundamental Causes of Disease." Extra issue, *Journal of Health and Social Behavior* 35e (1995): 80–94.

Littlejohn, Krystale. "Hormonal Contraceptive Use and Discontinuation Because of Dissatisfaction: Differences by Race and Education." *Demography* 49, no. 4 (2012): 1433–52.

———. "'It's Those Pills That Are Ruining Me': Gender and the Social Meanings of Hormonal Contraceptive Side Effects." *Gender and Society* 27, no. 6 (2013): 843–63.

Logan, Cassandra, Emily Holcombe, Jennifer Manlove, and Suzanne Ryan. *The Consequences of Unintended Childbearing: A White Paper.* Washington,

DC: National Campaign to Prevent Teen and Unplanned Pregnancy and Child Trends, 2007.

Lorber, Judith. *Paradoxes of Gender.* Binghamton, NY: Yale University Press, 1994.

Lowe, Pam. "Contraception and Heterosex: An Intimate Relationship." *Sexualities* 8, no. 1 (2005): 75–92. First published online February 1, 2005. https://doi.org/10.1177/1363460705049575.

Luker, Kristin. *Taking Chances: Abortion and the Decision Not to Contracept.* Berkeley: University of California Press, 1975.

———. *When Sex Goes to School.* New York: W.W. Norton, 2006.

Luna, Zakiya. "From Rights to Justice: Women of Color Changing the Face of US Reproductive Rights Organizing." *Societies without Borders* 4 (2009): 343–65.

Luna, Zakiya, and Kristin Luker. "Reproductive Justice." *Annual Review of Law and Social Science* 9 (2013): 327–52.

Manchikanti Gomez, Anu, Emily S. Mann, and Vanessa Torres. "'It Would Have Control over Me Instead of Me Having Control': Intrauterine Devices and the Meaning of Reproductive Freedom." *Critical Public Health* 28, no. 2 (2018): 190–200. First published online May 26, 2017.

Manlove, Jennifer, Kate Welti, Megan Barry, Kristen Peterson, Erin Schelar, and Elizabeth Wildsmith. "Relationship Characteristics and Contraceptive Use among Young Adults." *Perspectives on Sexual and Reproductive Health* 43, no. 2 (2011): 119–28.

Mann, Emily S., and Patrick R. Grzanka. "Agency-without-Choice: The Visual Rhetorics of Long-Acting Reversible Contraception Promotion." *Symbolic Interaction* 41, no. 3 (2018): 334–56. https://doi.org/10.1002/symb.349.

Marston, Cicely, and Eleanor King. "Factors That Shape Young People's Sexual Behaviour: A Systematic Review." *Lancet* 368, no. 9,547 (November 4, 2006): 1581–86. https://doi.org/10.1016/S0140-6736(06)69662-1.

Martinez, Gladys M., and Joyce C. Abma. "Sexual Activity and Contraceptive Use among Teenagers Aged 15–19 in the United States, 2015–2017." NCHS Data Brief, no. 366 (2020). Hyattsville, MD: National Center for Health Statistics.

Masters, N. Tatiana, Diane M. Morrison, Katherine Querna, Erin A. Casey, and Blair Beadnell. "Correlates of Young Men's Intention to Discuss Birth Control with Female Partners." *Perspectives on Sexual and Reproductive Health* 49, no. 1 (2017): 37–43.

Miller, Frank C. "Ten Goals for the American College of Obstetricians and Gynecologists for the First Decade of the Next Millennium." *Obstetrics and Gynecology* 95, no. 1 (2000): 1–5.

Mills, C. Wright. *The Sociological Imagination.* New York: Oxford University Press, 2000. First published 1959.

Mollborn, Stefanie. *Mixed Messages: Norms and Social Control around Teen Sex and Pregnancy.* New York: Oxford University Press, 2017.

Mora, Richard. "'Do It for All Your Pubic Hairs!' Latino Boys, Masculinity, and Puberty." *Gender and Society* 26, no. 3 (2012): 433–60.

Mosher, William D., Jo Jones, and Joyce C. Abma. "Intended and Unintended Births in the United States: 1982–2010." Atlanta: US Department of Health and Human Services, Centers for Disease Control and Prevention, National Center for Health Statistics, 2012.

Mosher, William D., Gladys M. Martinez, Anjani Chandra, Joyce C. Abma, and Stephanie J. Willson. "Use of Contraception and Use of Family Planning Services in the United States: 1982–2002." *Advance Data from Vital and Health Statistics* 350, no. 1 (2004): 1–36.

Nack, Adina. *Damaged Goods: Women Living with Incurable Sexually Transmitted Diseases.* Philadelphia: Temple University Press, 2008.

Nakano Glenn, Evelyn. "The Social Construction and Institutionalization of Gender and Race." In *Revisioning Gender,* edited by Myra Marx Ferree, Judith Lorber, and Beth B. Hess, 3–43. Thousand Oaks, CA: Sage, 1999.

Nelson, Jennifer. *More than Medicine: A History of the Feminist Women's Health Movement.* New York: New York University Press, 2015.

Oaks, Laury. *Giving Up Baby: Safe Haven Laws, Motherhood, and Reproductive Justice.* New York: New York University Press, 2015.

———. "Manhood and Meaning in the Marketing of the 'Male Pill.'" In *Reconceiving the Second Sex: Men, Masculinity, and Reproduction,* edited by Marcia C. Inhorn, Tine Tjørnhøj-Thomsen, Helene Goldberg, and Maruska la Cour Mosegaard, 139–59. New York: Berghahn Books, 2009.

Orenstein, Peggy. *Girls & Sex: Navigating the Complicated New Landscape.* New York: HarperCollins, 2016. https://doi.org/10.1177/0162243903259190.

Oudshoorn, Nelly. "Imagined Men: Representations of Masculinities in Discourses on Male Contraceptive Technology." In *Bodies of Technology: Women's Involvement with Reproductive Medicine,* edited by Ann Rudinow Saetnan, Nelly Oudshoorn, and Marta Kirejszyk, 123–45. Columbus: Ohio State University, 2000.

———. *The Male Pill.* Durham, NC: Duke University Press, 2003.

Oudshoorn, Nelly, Els Rommes, and Marcelle Stienstra. "Configuring the User as Everybody: Gender and Design Cultures in Information and Communication Technologies." *Science, Technology, and Human Values* 29, no. 1 (January 1, 2004): 30–63.

PATH, UNFPA. "Female Condom: A Powerful Tool for Protection." Seattle, WA: PATH, UNFPA, 2006.

Pazol, Karen, Michael R. Kramer, and Carol J. Hogue. "Condoms for Dual Protection: Patterns of Use with Highly Effective Contraceptive Methods." *Public Health Reports* 125, no. 2 (2010): 208–17.

Peipert, Jeffrey F., Qiuhong Zhao, Jenifer E. Allsworth, Emiko Petrosky, Tessa Madden, David Eisenberg, and Gina Secura. "Continuation and Satisfaction of Reversible Contraception." *Obstetrics and Gynecology* 117, no. 5 (2011): 1,105–13.

PerryUndem, *Contraceptives and Policy through a Gender Lens: Results from a National Survey Conducted by PerryUndem 17. PerryUndem Research Communication* (March 2017). https://www.scribd.com/document/342699692/PerryUndem-Gender-and-Birth-Control-Access-Report.

Price, Kimala. "What Is Reproductive Justice?: How Women of Color Activists Are Redefining the Pro-choice Paradigm." *Meridians: Feminism, Race, Transnationalism* 10, no. 2 (2010): 42–65.

Reagan, Leslie J. *When Abortion Was a Crime: Women, Medicine, and Law in the United States, 1867–1973.* Berkeley: University of California Press, 1997.

Reece, Michael, Debby Herbenick, Vanessa Schick, Stephanie A. Sanders, Brian Dodge, and J. Dennis Fortenberry. "Condom Use Rates in a National Probability Sample of Males and Females Ages 14 to 94 in the

United States." *Journal of Sexual Medicine* 7, no. s5 (2010): 266–76. https://doi.org/10.1111/j.1743-6109.2010.02017.x.

Reed, Joanna, Paula England, Krystale Littlejohn, Brooke Conroy Bass, and Mónica L. Caudillo. "Consistent and Inconsistent Contraception among Young Women: Insights from Qualitative Interviews." *Family Relations* 63, no. 2 (2014): 244–58.

Reeves, Richard V., and Eleanor Krause. "What's Stopping American Men from Getting Vasectomies?" *Social Mobility Memos* (blog). Brookings, October 14, 2016. https://www.brookings.edu/blog/social-mobility-memos/2016/10/14/whats-stopping-american-men-from-getting-vasectomies/.

Renzi, Cristina, Stephen R. Tabet, Jason A. Stucky, Niles Eaton, Anne S. Coletti, Christina M. Surawicz, S. Nicholas Agoff, Patrick J. Heagerty, Michael Gross, and Connie L. Celum. "Safety and Acceptability of the Reality Condom for Anal Sex among Men Who Have Sex with Men." *AIDS* (London) 17, no. 5 (March 28, 2003): 727–31. https://doi.org/10.1097/00002030-200303280-00011.

Roberts, Dorothy E. *Killing the Black Body: Race, Reproduction, and the Meaning of Liberty.* New York: Pantheon Books, 2014. First published 1997.

Ross, Loretta. "Understanding Reproductive Justice: Transforming the Pro-choice Movement." *Off Our Backs* 36, no. 4 (2006): 14–19.

Ross, Loretta, Sarah L. Brownlee, Dixon Dazon Diallo, Luz Rodriguez, and Latina Roundtable. "The 'SisterSong Collective': Women of Color, Reproductive Health and Human Rights." *American Journal of Health Studies* 17, no. 2 (2001): 79–88.

Ross, Loretta, Erika Derkas, Whitney Peoples, Lynn Roberts, and Pamela Bridgewater, eds. *Radical Reproductive Justice: Foundation, Theory, Practice, Critique.* New York: Feminist Press, 2017.

Ross, Loretta, and Rickie Solinger. *Reproductive Justice: An Introduction.* Berkeley: University of California Press, 2017.

Rubin, Gayle. "The Traffic in Women: Notes on the 'Political Economy' of Sex." In *Toward an Anthropology of Women,* edited by Rayna R. Reiter, 157–210. New York: Monthly Review Press, 1975.

Santelli, John, Roger Rochat, Kendra Hatfield-Timajchy, Brenda Colley Gilbert, Kathryn Curtis, Rebecca Cabral, Jennifer S. Hirsch, and Laura

Schieve. "The Measurement and Meaning of Unintended Pregnancy." *Perspectives on Sexual and Reproductive Health* 35, no. 2 (2003): 94–101.

Schoen, Johanna. *Choice and Coercion: Birth Control, Sterilization, and Abortion in Public Health and Welfare*. Chapel Hill: University of North Carolina Press, 2005.

Schonbrun, Zach. "XOXO Campaign: Will It Spell Profit or Trouble for Condom Maker?" *New York Times*, April 23, 2017. https://www.nytimes.com/2017/04/23/business/media/xoxo-campaign-will-it-spell-profit-or-trouble-for-condom-maker.html.

Sedgh, Gilda, Susheela Singh, and Rubina Hussain. "Intended and Unintended Pregnancies Worldwide in 2012 and Recent Trends." *Studies in Family Planning* 45, no. 3 (2014): 301–14.

Sewell, William H, Jr. "A Theory of Structure: Duality, Agency, and Transformation." *American Journal of Sociology* 98, no. 1 (1992): 1–29.

Shtulman, Andrew. *Scienceblind: Why Our Intuitive Theories about the World Are So Often Wrong*. New York: Basic Books, 2017.

Silliman, Jael. "Policing the National Body: Sex, Race, and Criminalization." Introduction to *Policing the National Body: Sex, Race, and Criminalization*, edited by Jael Silliman and Anannya Bhattacharjee, ix–xxix. Cambridge, MA: South End Press, 2002.

Silliman, Jael, Marlene Gerber Fried, Loretta Ross, and Elena R. Gutierrez. *Undivided Rights: Women of Color Organize for Reproductive Justice*. Cambridge, MA: South End Press, 2004.

Smith, Andrea. "Beyond Pro-choice versus Pro-life: Women of Color and Reproductive Justice." *NWSA* 17, no. 1 (2005): 119–40.

Sobo, Elisa Janine. *Choosing Unsafe Sex: AIDS-Risk Denial among Disadvantaged Women*. Philadelphia: University of Pennsylvania Press, 1995.

Solinger, Rickie. *Pregnancy and Power: A Short History of Reproductive Politics in America*. New York: New York University Press, 2005.

———. *Wake Up Little Susie: Single Pregnancy and Race Before Roe v. Wade*. 3rd ed. New York: Routledge, 2000.

Sonfield, Adam, Kinsey Hasstedt, and Rachel Benson Gold. *Moving Forward: Family Planning in the Era of Health Reform*. New York: Guttmacher Institute, 2014.

Stern, Lisa. "Planning the Unplanned Pregnancy." Paper presented at the North American Forum on Family Planning, Chicago, IL, November 2015.

Takeshita, Chikako. *The Global Biopolitics of the IUD: How Science Constructs Contraceptive Users and Women's Bodies.* Cambridge, MA: MIT Press, 2012.

Tavory, Iddo, and Ann Swidler. "Condom Semiotics: Meaning and Condom Use in Rural Malawi." *American Sociological Review* 74, no. 2 (2009): 171–89.

Terry, Gareth, and Virginia Braun. "'It's Kind of Me Taking Responsibility for These Things': Men, Vasectomy and Contraceptive Economies." *Feminism and Psychology* 21, no. 4 (2011): 477–95.

Timmermans, Stefan, and Iddo Tavory. "Theory Construction in Qualitative Research: From Grounded Theory to Abductive Analysis." *Sociological Theory* 30, no. 3 (2012): 167–86. First published September 10, 2012. https://doi.org/10.1177/0735275112457914.

Tone, Andrea. *Devices and Desires: A History of Contraceptives in America.* New York: Hill and Wang, 2001.

Trussell, James. "The Cost of Unintended Pregnancy in the United States." *Contraception* 75, no. 3 (2007): 168–70.

Trussell, James, Nathaniel Henry, Fareen Hassan, Alexander Prezioso, Amy Law, and Anna Filonenko. "Burden of Unintended Pregnancy in the United States: Potential Savings with Increased Use of Long-Acting Reversible Contraception." *Contraception* 87, no. 2 (2013): 154–61.

Twenge, Jean M., Ryne A. Sherman, and Brooke E. Wells. "Changes in American Adults' Sexual Behavior and Attitudes, 1972–2012." *Archives of Sexual Behavior* 44, no. 8 (November 2015): 2273–85. https://doi.org/10.1007/s10508-015-0540-2.

Twine, France Winddance. *Outsourcing the Womb: Race, Class, and Gestational Surrogacy in a Global Market.* New York: Routledge, 2011.

United Nations. *Report of the Fourth World Conference on Women: Beijing 4–15 September 1995.* New York: United Nations, 1996. http://www.un.org/womenwatch/daw/beijing/pdf/Beijing%20full%20report%20E.pdf.

US Department of Health and Human Services, Office of Disease Prevention and Health Promotion. *Healthy People 2020* (blog). Washington, DC: US Department of Health and Human Services, n.d. https://www.healthypeople.gov/2020/topics-objectives/topic/family-planning#ten.

Waggoner, Miranda R. *The Zero Trimester: Pre-pregnancy Care and the Politics of Reproductive Risk.* Oakland: University of California Press, 2017.

West, Candace, and Don H. Zimmerman. "Doing Gender." *Gender and Society* 1, no. 2 (June 1, 1987): 125–51. https://doi.org/10.1177/08912432870 01002002.

Wolitski, R. J., P. N. Halkitis, J. T. Parsons, and C. A. Gómez. "Awareness and Use of Untested Barrier Methods by HIV-Seropositive Gay and Bisexual Men." *AIDS Education and Prevention: Official Publication of the International Society for AIDS Education* 13, no. 4 (August 2001): 291–301. https:// doi.org/10.1521/aeap.13.4.291.21430.

Woodsong, Cynthia, and Helen P. Koo. "Two Good Reasons: Women's and Men's Perspectives on Dual Contraceptive Use." *Social Science and Medicine* 49, no. 5 (September 1, 1999): 567–80. https://doi.org/10.1016 /S0277-9536(99)00060-X.

Index

Black feminist epistemology, 143n48
Black feminist theory of knowledge,
47, 97
Black women: channeling into
prescription birth control use,
50–51; condom buying, bringing,
and use, 102–5, 106–8, 109–12,
114–15; condoms and STIs, 41–44;
gender expectations and
non-normative behavior, 17–18,
100, 102, 104, 106, 107–8, 114,
116, 122–23; methods used, 105–6;
as participants in study, 140; and
the pill, 114–15; prescription birth
control, 50–51, 106–9, 110–11,
114–16; racial stereotypes and
reproduction, 98; responsibility
for prevention of pregnancies,
110–11; social contexts in
pregnancies, 99, 100; two
methods use, 114–16
Black women and less advantaged
women: in gendered compulsory
birth control, 3–4; and gender
expectations, 98–100; and gender
inequality in birth control, 122;
and paid work, 101–2; pregnancies
and social contexts, 99–100, 122;
and prevention of pregnancies,
122; resistance to gendered
behavior in birth control use,
17–18, 100; unintended pregnancy, 6, 117–19
Brianne (participant), 61–62

Carolina (participant), 28–29, 37
Carolyn (participant), 56, 90–91
"causal chain," 100

Centers for Disease Control and
Prevention, 7, 20–21, 39–40, 126
chlamydia cases, 40
Cindy (participant), 87–89
Claire (participant), 41, 86–87, 95–96
Collins, Patricia Hill, 125
conception. *See* pregnancy
condoms (external): avoidance and
resistance by men, 43, 76, 77, 78,
79–82, 83–84, 86–89, 103–5,
107–10, 111–13; and Black women,
41–44, 102–5, 106–8, 109–12,
114–15; buying or bringing by
women, 32–33, 35–37, 50, 51, 102–5,
109; correct use and knowledge
about, 37–39; dislike by women,
31–32; effectiveness, 109, 125, 126,
127; encouragement to use, 128,
129; financial help for, 25, 26; free
supply, 128, 129; and gender,
20–23, 24–25, 26, 28–29, 30, 31, 38,
51, 113; gendered compulsory birth
control, 76, 77, 78, 79–82, 83–89;
gender inequality in birth control,
24, 128; and language, 130; latex
allergy, 102; learning by women,
19, 23–27; made for women, 22;
male partners' views and
dissatisfaction, 27–29, 30–31, 32; as
"men's method," 16, 22–23, 29,
30–32, 45, 88–89, 113; as not
gendered method, 20, 30, 113; and
the pill (switch/transition to), 1–2,
49, 75, 86–87, 129; and the pill (use
in tandem), 29–30, 84–86;
provision by men, 33–37; public
health campaigns, 126–27;
reliability and alternatives for

gender *(continued)*
131–32, 133; as concept, 10–11; and
condoms (external), 20–23, 24–25,
26, 28–29, 30, 31, 38, 51, 113; and
contraception, 47–48, 99, 119,
124–25; education about, 130–32;
expectations (*See* gender expectations); intersectional analysis, 14,
100, 101, 121–22; and knowledge
about contraception, 38–39; and
language, 130; in learning and
socialization, 19–22, 23–24, 121,
131–32; and methods of contraception, 2–3, 20–21; and pregnancy,
90, 91, 93–95; and prevention of
pregnancies, 124–25, 126; and public
health, 20–21; and race, 14, 99,
101–2, 122; reduction of differences,
101–2; and reproductively just
vision for the future, 133–34; vs. sex,
10–11; and sex education, 23–24,
131; as social accomplishment, 101;
and social contexts, 14, 101–2, 122,
124–25; and violence, 116–17
gendered compulsory birth control:
author's experience, 96–97; Black
and less advantaged women, 3–4;
and condom use by men, 76, 77,
78, 79–82, 83–89; consequences, 3,
4, 15–16, 73, 83; description and
approaches, 3–4, 17, 74; and
doctors, 82–83; examples, 74–77;
gender inequality in birth control,
74–83, 97; and hegemony, 97;
interruption of perpetuation, 100;
and men's needs, 77–79; and
pregnancies, 83–88, 95; and
reproductive autonomy of

women, 3, 97, 124; and reproductive justice, 124; social acceptance, 121–22; solutions for, 124–34
gendered division of labor. *See*
division of labor
gender expectations: and Black
women, 17–18, 100, 102, 104, 106,
107–8, 114, 116, 122–23; and
hormonal birth control, 57–58, 59,
113–14, 121; and less advantaged
women, 98–100; and prescription
birth control, 50–51, 52–53, 57, 73,
74–76, 80, 83–84, 100, 107–8,
113–14; and white women, 112–13
gender inequality in birth control: as
argument in *Just Get on the Pill*, 3,
14; for Black and less advantaged
women, 122; and condoms, 24, 128;
and effectiveness of contraceptives, 125–26; gendered compulsory birth control, 74–83, 97; harm
from, 133; and pregnancy, 99;
reduction strategies, 128–29; and
social structures, 74, 122; and
unintended pregnancy, 118
Gina (participant), 57, 58, 82–83
gonorrhea cases, 40
Grzanka, Patrick, 59
Gutman, Matthew, 128

health clinics, and hygiene products,
129
health insurance, 127–28
Healthy People 2020 public health
goals, 7
hegemony, 97, 101
heterosexuality, and gender
ideology, 47–48

less advantaged women, 6,
117–19; data on, 6; definition, 2;
and public health, 7–8; in US, 5–6
UN World Conference on Women in
Beijing (1995), 12

Valentina (participant), 41, 56
Vanessa (participant), 49–50, 51, 64,
85–86
vasectomy, 127–28
violence against women, 116–17

weight gain, 60, 61–63, 65–66
white women: methods used,
106; non-normative gender
behavior, 112–13; as participants
in study, 140; pregnancies in
participants, 99
withdrawal method, use of, 105, 110
women of color, and reproductive
justice, 123–24. *See also* Black
women; Black women and less
advantaged women
"women's method" and prescription
birth control: as category, 48–49,
120; consequences, 83; and men's
needs, 78, 79; overview, 16–17, 45,
47–49

XOXO condom, 22

"yes means yes," 131

Founded in 1893,
UNIVERSITY OF CALIFORNIA PRESS
publishes bold, progressive books and journals
on topics in the arts, humanities, social sciences,
and natural sciences—with a focus on social
justice issues—that inspire thought and action
among readers worldwide.

The UC PRESS FOUNDATION
raises funds to uphold the press's vital role
as an independent, nonprofit publisher, and
receives philanthropic support from a wide
range of individuals and institutions—and from
committed readers like you. To learn more, visit
ucpress.edu/supportus.